A Doctored Life

From Homeless to Harvard

Jimmy Moss, MD

Thank You Tracy!

pieces.

This book is dedicated to my daughters:
Tamara, Sierra, Jayla, and Amaya.
"Blood doesn't make us family, accountability does. "
Love, Dad

introduction:

Before the money. Before the luxury cars. Before the million-dollar homes and Arhaus Madrone leather sofas with color coordinated pillows. Before Harvard and Mayo Clinic. Before graduating medical school with honors. Before becoming a father and community pillar, lauded for efforts I would much rather remain a memory than become memorialized. Before my collegiate academic advisor, Mrs. Anderson, asked me the one question that started it all. Before Section 8 housing and homelessness. Before I traded in my childhood Marvel Comic cards for my first job at twelve. Before ever considering a semblance of a plan that would somehow afford me a better life than the one I entertained as a child, I was just a kid.

A black kid. A smart black kid who grew up poor like a lot of other smart black kids, so my story is no different. I wish I could tell you that I am exclusively writing this to motivate others, to be an inspiration to someone going through something, but I can't. I don't believe motivation can be forced, no more than I believe inspiration can be *entirely* delivered via social media posts and perfectly timed memes. Motivation and Inspiration are difficult concepts to explore because they are found within the crevices of life experiences. They are personal ideals that perimeter our choices and lives. Since no two people equally reflect each other, whatever motivates and inspires them can only be mirrored—never refracted. I once started to read a book about motivation, but never finished it. Yet, I often find myself not eating extra cookies because I'm convinced that I need to cut back, lose weight, and live longer to spend more time with my smart black kids.

These, Motivation and Inspiration, are manifested as personal experiences that are born of untapped mettle we happen upon, discovering them only when the right moment introduces itself. Writing this book does not feel like my moment, but maybe reading it is yours. Maybe you are, as I have been numerous times in my life, very close to turning the page toward a better you. Maybe you are looking for a push or are in search of something to inspire someone else to embrace their individual greatness. Maybe you will learn that you and I are not much different at all—even though I have my story and you have yours.

This commonality we share as humans is one of the reasons why I wrote this book. The other (primary) reason is the hope that, one day, my daughters may gain something from it that helps them better understand our connection. I think we use other people's journeys and testimonies as jumping points to re-configure our own efforts. This same commonality is also unknowingly abiding within the core of the prematurity that outlines my young children's idea of themselves. If they find clarity when they stumble upon these pages later in life, then I will consider this literary effort worthwhile. I, moreover, hope that in reading about these chapters exploring my life, you will begin to examine your own vulnerabilities. What is it about your past that has indirectly guided your future? What motivates you? What inspires you? What created that small voice in your head that may, or may not, have given you the boost you needed to finish a pressing assignment, apply for that out of state job, avoid picking up that extra cookie on the breakroom table, or even write a book?

We all have a story. Although we often lean on the experiences of others, I do not think we necessarily need other people's stories to motivate and inspire us; we can tap into our own. I challenge you to become your own novelist and narrator. I encourage you to not be afraid of reexploring the life you've traveled, nor let your journey prevent you from continuing toward the better life you are embracing. If my "being open" moves you to do the same, then I hope your encounter is as eventful as mine has been.

a fight.

K ids should never see their mother beaten; it disrupts balance. We all come from a mother, so to watch the very source of your existence being abused or mishandled tips the scale a little toward darkness, a deep-seated bitterness. You begin to ask yourself, "Why is she so powerless and so frail?" The more questions you ask, the more you begin to isolate yourself on an island of acceptance: This is her, so this is me. I am powerless, I am frail. I am little, but big enough to appreciate just how little I am in these moments- and I don't like it. You never question why someone is beating her; you never ask yourself if she did anything wrong or if she is deserving of her wounds that will eventually become "remember what happened to me" scars.

What you do, instead, is cry. You get angry, not knowing that anger never erases memories and pain, it enhances them. You try to process these ugly occurrences with rapidly growing brain cells that are still untangling through small glances of your view of things, still searching for a landing spot in time. Eventually you dare yourself to blink, and in that moment "it goes away." The beatings. The thinking. The pain. The reality that this is your beating, as well; your fists-less fight, your collection of unused punches. She is not losing, you are. There is no balance, just a stream of evolving emotions and images that are covered from your ability to process them during a small fraction of time in between blinks. Eyes close and open; screams fade and then return. You try to hold onto something, physical and firm, something nearby and bigger than you because you are losing everything else. And before you've untangled enough neurons to plug yourself into what is unfathomably occurring, someone else's ill-balanced voice awakens you before you can reopen your eyes.

"Get off my momma!" my brother screamed as he swung his plastic guitar against Ulysses' back.

It shattered. Not just into little pieces, but also into chunks- shiny chunks with little blue stars and sparkling red outlining them. Still holding the neck of his broken instrument, face soaked with puddles of anger, Jerald swung again. The plastic guitar strings stretched and unveiled his anger across the warm air being pushed down from a dusty ceiling fan. He was younger, and at this point a little smaller, than me, but his tears were a lot larger—as was his heart. Nothing happened though, nothing stopped. Just more scattered pieces he would later get yelled at for not picking up quickly enough to resolve any lingering disappointment my mother had about what we were being asked to absorb hours earlier. Her sweat and blood stained Ulysses' fists, which only paused long enough for him to catch his breath. Hard breaths; spit dripping from his words. His promises to bring more harm were laced with heroin-like curse words and more breathing. The pictures on each wall didn't move but they were trying to stay quiet and still, shying away from the heaviness of pain being thrust into air.

I, also, was too scared to move, but I saw everything. My mom was shoved into a corner while Ulysses' massive arms swung forcefully against her face. With every punch, a deafening thump filled the room. I couldn't hear her cry; I honestly thought she was dead until she moved. Her foot kicked out from under the cloak of his shadow. When it did, I gasped. I selfishly didn't want her to move. I was glad she was not dead, but I was afraid that him seeing her "alive" would make him more upset or stronger, or not care about breathing.

I can't recall what happened after that. Where he went, or what she said or felt. I remember being in the car though, her face swollen and bloodied. It looked like she had cherry fingernail polish pouring down from her eyes; yet, the deep melanin in her cheeks held the redness of pain at bay. Although I was the oldest, I sat in the back seat. We usually fought over riding shotgun, but I got dibs most of the time because my mom felt like, as the oldest, I needed to be up front, to pay attention in case something happened. I was bright enough to be geographically observant, even at nine years old. That day, however, I didn't want to sit next to her. I was still numb from the thumping noise. Each punch sounded like a hammer hitting the arm of a couch; dull, but annoyingly noticeable. Staring at her blood reminded me of what blood tasted like; a lingering metallic indifference that almost immediately invited your other senses to the occasion. I wondered if she could taste it, or if tasting it made her upset and quiet—a quietness she selflessly shared for most of the car ride.

She looked at me a few times thru the rearview mirror; caught me staring at the anger underlining her pain that was both familiar and somewhat foreign. I didn't know whether she wanted me to see her face or if she was embarrassed that I could. My brother sat up front, head bobbing in cadence with every unfilled pothole South Florida gifted us after we begged the sky for rain. All of us were quiet at first, even my sister, Jessica, behind her tears and shock. She was too little to really know what was contouring her future; her genetic womanhood was very much asleep but still listening. Underneath her unblemished sun-kissed cheekbones were the fixed beginnings of pain being carved into place. This is how men and women resolve conflicts and arguments; this is the norm. This is okay because, well, when has it ever "not" been okay? This wasn't the first time we saw our mother get beaten, wasn't the last either. This time felt different though; like it should have been enough, but we knew better. Men beat women, we thought. Maybe it wasn't supposed to happen but when it did (at least when we saw it), it left us with the same feeling you had whenever you saw a sibling getting an ass whooping: glad it's not me.

As we got closer to Ms. Ruby's house, my mother started crying, loudly, repeatedly banged the steering wheel and yelled—new tears softening the crusted older ones mixed with sweat and dried blood. Her words were muffled under that thumping sound still in my head, rhythmically echoing with flickering images of shiny guitar pieces scattered all over the living room floor—blue stars with red lines around them. She carried her theatrics to Ms. Ruby's front door, my siblings and I in tow, a few shameful steps behind her. Trying to keep up, we hurried while coyishly aiming to avoid stepping on the cracks in the driveway. It was long and only narrow enough for the old Buick that was filled with stacks of newspapers and bags of whatever people kept inside of old Buicks in narrow driveways. The cracks were wide enough to avoid but presented a challenge because some of them had little flowers sprouting from the soil the asphalt purposely covered. Yellow flowers with hovering bumblebees; red flowers with none. I almost finished my imaginary obstacle course mistake free until I heard my mother yelling, "Look at my face! Look at what your son did to my face!!"

Coldly, Ms. Ruby stared at her. Her eyes were deep and brown but were now sunken into a red sea of disturbed resentment. She liked my mom, but hated that her son liked my mom, as well. To her, my mom was a ride to church and the flea market, but also the fast heifer with three kids and no real means to enforce their dad to work long hard hours and take care of them like her son was currently doing. Joyce + Ulysses' weekly paycheck equaled Ulysses minus Ms. Ruby getting her fair share of her son's pre-beer money. The math was bad enough, but now the woman stealing her side cash was standing on her front steps, in broad daylight, disturbing the silence that old people savored whenever kids were still asleep and the sun was barely awake. She stood there, quiet and unmoved by the noise, the blood, the new tears, or the kids, homely dressed, who gazed up at her with a pity that ran deeper than the creased wrinkles in her house dress. I don't remember any police being called or what my mom was wearing. I can't recall why she wasn't crying when she left the house, during most of the drive or when she caught me staring at her in the rearview mirror. But I remember Ms. Ruby's house dress. Light pink with little yellow flowers; pretty flowers with ugly wrinkles. I also remember her words, how slowly they came out and how seriously she meant them.

"Girl don't come 'round here with that foolishness. You knew whatchu' were dealing with when you met'em."

They went back and forth, but I stopped listening because she was right. My mother knew. Ulysses was just a name of the same type of guy she dealt with for years. Big Jimmy. Dwight. Reggie. Matt. Terry. Vince. Mark. Harry. Bud. That one man who left money on her dresser (that she never let me count) after he left without speaking. Some were friends. Some were lovers. All were drinkers; same drama, same story—same mom. We knew. The arguing continued, even as the distance between them expanded and the front door closed. We ignored the cracks and followed our heated mother back to the car without any sound announcing our willingness to be unnoticed. As she pulled off, I stared at the small, red flower I accidently stepped on trying to sidestep the last crack before my efforts to avoid breaking my mother's back were rudely interrupted. I sat in the front seat on the way home; body stiffened with embarrassment while I faced the passenger window, eyes fixated on how ignorant the world was to all the hurt inside of our car as we headed home. I didn't want to sit in the front, but no one called shotgun, so it defaulted to me. Initially Jerald probably figured he bested me by not having to sit next to mom; however, he had to deal with her eyes in the rearview mirror this time—and that was fine with me.

She made us clean up when we arrived home. My grandmother came over and did her usual, unwelcomed "I told you so," followed with head shakes and "Jesus" sighs. My brother got into trouble for asking for a new guitar; no beatings, just words, nasty accusations as if it was his fault for swinging it at Ulysses. It made us both upset—him, because he liked that guitar; me, because I felt like she was basically saying, "This wasn't your fight, it was mine."

I hated when she did that. She did it a lot, boldly assuming that because we were kids, things like this didn't affect us. Fights. Drunken arguments. Ex-felon boyfriends giving us "advice on how to be men." I hated her for all of it when I was a kid. I blamed her for the fights and lack of awareness, I just didn't know how to say it, nor did I have the space to discuss it. I hated her for taking us to Ms. Ruby's house that day; for letting us see her aimlessly trying to prove to her womanizing husband's mother that her "son wasn't worth a damn." I hated how stupid I felt, being her son that day, when Ms. Ruby said her piece and left it at that. I hated wiping her blood off the side of the TV, which was next to that corner I thought she died in. I hated that my brother was as mad as I was, but for far less thoughtful reasons.

"She better get me a new guitar," Jerald said angrily under his breath. She never did.

Toys were never replaced, nor were toys ever recovered from department store layaway containers we excitedly hoped would show up at the house—gift wrapped with our names written on the packages. My mother's *J* was distinctively hers; unable to be forged or copied. If she signed something, you knew it came from *Joyce. Joyce Jackson. Joyce Moss. Joyce Richardson. Joyce Broughton.* She loved her name and wrote it down constantly. I don't think there was a measure of vanity behind it, but rather a sort of newness we all covet at times. A new name meant a new beginning. A new boyfriend or husband meant a new chance at love. A new address was, well, a new house or home, or sometimes just a place you resided at and waited for presents to arrive.

Our gift? All *J*s, written with distinctive swirls and curves. After Big *Jimmy* left, it was only *Joyce*, little *Jimmy, Jerald, Jessica*, and whoever else my mom invited into the pictures. None of their names started with a *J*, though; none of them stuck around long enough for me to even care. But they all left scars, some physical and some intangible from emotional wars they invisibly fought by not sticking around. Some of them took their last names back from my mom when they left, and sometimes it felt like she wished they would have taken her with them as well.

2

on call.

The door didn't close shut. As my attending and I listened to the Palliative Care team outline what they discussed with Mr. Jay's wife, all I could hear were her tears. The ventilator's rhythmic echoes sounded like a tiring Darth Vader breathing twenty-four breaths per minute, at a fixed tidal volume and positive end-expiratory pressure of 12; each fully oxygenated breath interrupting her sniffling. I wanted to pay attention, but not listening to her pain felt more costly. After rounds, I circled back and found the door no longer ajar. My knock was answered by a welcoming voice. Upon entering, she stood there, facing me with a confidence that felt shaken and battered. Her voice quivered with a "here we go again" lingering tone, as if a doctor entering the room somehow brought her the same feeling when they left the room: more nothingness.

More questions about dying instead of healing, comfort instead of cures. She knew he was suffering, but she wasn't sure if he was suffering more from his acute myeloid leukemia blast crisis or the volume of hope she was daily being asked to surrender. A large man, dark skin covered in a veil of illness, his atrophied face contoured puddles of light around the shadows of his facial bones. He was both there and not there; tubes and catheters becoming more and more present as his absence started to arrive. Sick people have a look to them. It's hard to verbalize but eerily noticeable. His wife stood there, staring at him, waiting for him. The heaviness of his illnesses weighed less than what her eyes were absorbing. Ventilators. IV poles with medications infusing via pumps that felt colder as their numbers increased. He was sick, she understood that, but the gravity of multiorgan failure is hard to fathom. Sickness revealing itself through an imbalance of red and black numbers on lab reports. It was as if his livelihood somehow transitioned from an abstract prism of the man she had loved for a number of years, to the concrete reality of that number being replaced.

"Eight years," she answered. "Well, we've been together eleven years, but married eight. And a half."

I was trying to make small talk. In my brief time as a physician, I found that asking small personal questions was a convenient ice breaker when your fund of knowledge was limited. I couldn't explain the nuances of his treatment regimen, but I could spark a decent convo; listen and not add to the interruption. So, I did. She told me stories that felt honest and kind, shared memories about how his sense of humor mirrored his stubbornness. She started to blame herself for his condition. After nagging him to "see a doctor" once he noticed himself sleeping more and more, she said he would crack a joke and blame his fatigue on late night intimacy or her keeping him up watching Crime TV.

Her urges and obliges matched his jokes and uncanny knack of keeping her concerns at bay for about a year, until he had his first bout of pneumonia. Then his second. When he didn't seem to be improving after a few more urgent care visits, lab work was performed. Later that day a phone call came, informing Jay to be seen immediately for an elevated white blood cell (WBC) count. They both thought a high WBC was to be expected with an infection; however, his elevated cells were not mature enough to be of any use. Their number wasn't the issue, their immaturity was. They were poorly functioning. Just a bunch of cells designed to heal; yet, not participating in healing. But rather just bumming around, taking up space and drinking all the Kool-Aid. The urgent care physician advised Jay to visit the nearest ER, noting that more tests and studies needed to be performed. He was tired, but this time he obliged.

She held his hand tighter whenever she reached various points in the story of his journey, from abnormal lab work to "here." Random tangents when something reminded her of how they met in the Navy, or how they opted to not have kids so they could travel and see the world. Big plans on an Earth that felt small. A timeless couple, identifying with the fairytale of life, pixy dust, and champagne in Paris. She had pictures to prove her point; smiles pieced together by photo pixels that were color coded and dipped into rainbow perfection. No filters, just the shadow of love contrasted with highlights and a dramatic warmth that was more authentic than the thousands of words these images were worth to her.

"We felt like conquerors," she proclaimed, swiping through her phone's photo album, as Jay laid there without interrupting.

As my hospital shifts turned into two weeks, Mr. Jay was near the end of his life; his battle with cancer traded in for a larger and more ominous enemy: sepsis. In and of itself, it's not really a disease state, it's a syndrome. By definition, sepsis is life-threatening organ dysfunction due to a dysregulated host response to an infection. Jay, the host, had an immune system that was overwhelmingly compromised by cancer. Even in its weakened state, though, it became more dysregulated during its newest challenge against an infection, pneumonia. We administered antibiotics, supported failing organs, and intervened as best as we could; however, the spoils of death's victory were not willingly shared. There was a rich sadness when he passed away from the tears of Nursing teammates who were present when he was well enough to laugh and tell jokes, to the family members lining the hospital halls like Negro folk art paintings—hugging and embracing each other with a calm steadiness.

The family members were Jay's people, old and young, different sizes and mannerisms. Each had their own receptive pose they held rigidly close, as if movement was forbidden. After his body was taken to the morgue, many of them started shuffling toward red exit signs pointing to elevators that some- how never felt overcrowded during such moments. His wife stayed behind, awkwardly alone, trying to decipher what to do next. Standing there, a thir- ty-three-year-old new widow, she embarrassingly tried calling Jay's friends and siblings, who were a few floors below looking for their cars and rides home, to see which funeral home they preferred. She wasn't prepared for his death, but she felt like she should have been. Racing through her phone and googling mortuaries, one of the ICU nurses gave her a list of commonly used establishments in the city.

"Thank you," she replied. Folding the list in her hand after dialing the first number at the top. "Yes, umm. This is, umm, Mrs. W___. And, umm, my husband just passed away and I, umm, was wondering if you all… I don't know how this works. I'm sorry," placing the phone against her chest, waiting for the emotions to pass. "Yes, I am at Mayo, and his name is…"

She was from Texas, and when he was admitted, noted that they had planned to return there after Jay recovered. When he didn't, I assumed her plans didn't change, and by the way his family hurriedly left after he died, I didn't blame her. After securing a funeral home, she sat in his room, gathering his items, leaving behind Gatorades and guilty snacks she purchased earlier in the week when she was trying to trick herself into hunger.

I came by to pay my respects. I gave her a hug that I wasn't sure I was supposed to give but knew I would give—if that makes sense. I've hugged family members before, one-arm church embraces with quick pats on the back; however, this felt different. For the first time in my career, I experienced what it feels like to share the weight a person carries when they lose a loved one. It's a heaviness that is hard to describe; almost as if they are giving their burdens to you, not to carry but rather to understand. And for the first time, I understood, and it made sense. We are taught about death in medical school, but it's via the eyes of a disease state; the final chapter of a person's ailments, read numbingly out loud but only heard by a select few. That number varies. What never changes, however, is how personal it all becomes. The absence of sound, the haziness of memories, the suddenness of a reality no longer allowing you to ignore what you may have been bravely denying. All of it becomes no longer adaptable; all of it becomes personal. In that moment, I could appreciate how hard it must have been for her to *keep it all together*, especially around people who barely understood the parts.

Before I left, we chatted about a few aimless things. I knew she had more to say but couldn't find the words. Deep inside of my core arose this sense of responsibility. A part of me felt like, "I couldn't save her husband, but maybe I can somehow help her cope". Extending my cell number, I invited her to reach out if she ever had any questions later about his death, or if she ever needed to vent. At the beginning of residency, we were advised to never share our personal contact information with patients, or their family members. Yet, I felt obligated to her as if her husband and I were invisibly connected, and that it was my duty to help his widow get through these coming weeks—a time frame when death sinks in and can often drag you into a hole of depression.

I didn't hear from her for a week; I figured she found her support system and was on her way to the next stage of her life. Then one day, I received a text message from a Texas area code:

Hi, Dr Moss, sorry to bother. This is Jay's wife and I just wanted to thank you for everything. His service was beautiful. So many flowers, the message read.

Wow. Thanks for this message. I was wondering how everything went. Are you ok?

Yes. I am well. Thank you. My sister flew into town to help me sort things out. I am moving back to Texas in a few weeks. I can't stay here, it's too hard.

Oh, I understand. I am glad you have her. How long will she be here?

For a few weeks. Yes, she has been a huge help.

Nice! Well, I am glad you are doing well. I really am. Keep me posted.

I will. Mos def. Thank you, for everything. You all were awesome!

You're welcome.

Closure. That is how I justified it (i.e., our brief text sessions) in my head. My patient passed away. His wife needed more time to adjust to her new life without him. Hearing from her and knowing that she was pushing forward gave me a sense of completeness. I could not cure him, but my willingness to extend my concern beyond a hospital death summary in his chart was an amazing feeling. A few more weeks went by, and his wife texted me again; informing me that she finally made it to Texas and sent me a photo of her smiling with her new puppy—Jax. She named him after Jacksonville, Florida, noting that she wanted to have a positive memory of her time in the city. Since she and Jay never had kids, Jax gave her something to love and focus her attention toward.

The texting started to fade; time eventually exposed the lack of things for us to discuss. Our connection was via her husband; there were no bonds to realign or adjust, the communication was more professional than it was personal—at least for me it was. Even more, it was hard to talk about the reason we were even texting in the first place: him. It felt like the more I asked about him, the more I forced her to re-remember his passing, so I stopped asking. I felt unqualified to go beyond the basic "how are you coping?" topics. I discovered just how hard it was to speak once you realized that you bit off more than you could possibly chew. One day, however, she abruptly texted and asked if I could talk. The last time we communicated verbally was about three months prior, on the day he passed away, so I wasn't sure what there was to discuss. Both curious and surprised, I replied:

Sure. Is everything ok?

No. Not really. I'm sorry to bother you... I just got into an argument with my mother about Jay and I just needed to vent. I'm sorry—if you can't talk, I understand.

Two hours later, I called and was greeted with a quivery hello; the patchiness of a tearful conversation followed. She explained that her mother and Jay didn't get along; her mother never cared for her husband. When she and Jay first started dating, he was married to another woman who was carrying his child. After an ugly divorce, which had been marred by accusations of domestic abuse from his ex, Jay lost custodial rights because of a history "of violence." Consequently, he started drinking more, lost his position in the military for insubordination and substance abuse, and after life gave him nothing more to fight for, he started fighting her. At first it was a few scuffles, a few police calls that never ended in charges being filed, just warnings. But over time, things escalated. Shoves became punches, words became threats. Violent threats. One time, he showed up at her job and threw a chair through the window. That resulted in an arrest, and more liquor store visits.

When she was transferred to the Naval base in Jacksonville, she noted that he started to sober up a bit. They went to marital counseling; Jay went to Alcoholics Anonymous. She figured life was going to start turning around and then he started getting sick. She eventually circled back to her conversation with her mother. Her hopes were to use some of his life insurance money for a high school scholarship at his alma mater; however, her mother begged to differ. This led to an argument, then to a car drive, then to a text message to me, then to a phone call. And that phone call changed everything. I was happy she shared these things with me, but also saddened that she did. What was once a feeling of support and continuity, was now tainted with misguided disgusts. Domestic violence. An alcoholic abuser. A womanizer. My patient.

As a medical professional, I am not supposed to factor these things into how I feel about the ailing individuals under my umbrella of healing. In fact, we are only taught to feel positive emotions for those we care for, taught to always keep subjectivity tucked inside of white coat pockets, ready to be exchanged for an objective view of wellness. I didn't know Mr. Jay personally, but I carried him with me. I felt connected to his skin color, his voice, his laughter, and his suffering. I painted the insides of my eyelids the color of his red and black lab values during his hospital stay. I wrapped them over my eyes whenever I slept, trying to find patterns I could decipher, or trends that I could treat. The day he died, I left his room feeling defeated and somehow responsible for his wife's healing, as if he was my brother or my friend. Yet after that phone call, I felt ashamed. Angry at myself for getting "involved" beyond his hospital chart. Embarrassed that I couldn't pick up on the fact that the strength we all were asking him to use to "fight for his life", was the same strength he had forcibly stolen from his wife.

How do you care for a bad person? How do you separate emotions that were disgustingly stitched into the seams of the very fabric of your childhood from the adulthood traumas of another human? How do you balance that urge to pull negatively subjective thoughts from your white coat pocket, with the same hand you use to write orders with? I no longer viewed him as a patient; he became something affiliated with darkness and inner pain. Even in death he couldn't escape my judgment, my resentment. In medicine, we call it "counter-transference," the act of transferring our "feelings" about something or some-one, onto our patients—emotional entanglement. I stopped responding to his wife's texts; I found myself disappointed with her for not being upfront about his "badness," but that felt silly and childish. How he was as a person, or what he did before I met him, shouldn't matter in the scheme of providing care. My job, my duty, was to honor my oath: first, do no harm. However, in that moment I came face to face with a forgotten reality of my youth: a broken child, now, trying to be a strong man for a broken woman, who was wounded by a broken man. A vicious cycle. An unpretty truth. I eventually started to respond again, offered prayers and support from afar. After our communications faded again, I buried my feelings about the awkwardness surrounding it all with a quietness that still feels loud. I never gave out my number again during residency. I told myself, "Medicine is my calling, but I don't need a cell phone for that."

love songs.

The story goes as such: My mother and father met in, well, to be honest, I don't know how they met. All she told me was that he was persistent in his quest to date her, had a bowlegged stance, and was very hairy (so, a mammal with a childhood vitamin deficiency who never gave up on fulfilling his sexual pursuits—got it). She would tell me stories about my father, stories which rarely ended well. They were always recited with a cold "look at what he did to me??" victimlike hum that would push your face away from the phone whenever asked—so I didn't. He was a bad guy with some "good in him," but definitely a lot bad. They split sometime in the mid-80s, maybe 85, 86, etc. It wasn't a sudden shift, more of a gradual one. Big Jimmy was in and out of jail for petty crimes mixed with serious offenses. We never talked about him "not being there," he just wasn't around much. When he was around it wasn't memorable, and the parts I do remember are negatively biased. Other than a shared name and some ill-tempered mannerisms buried under *genes* I hardly wear, he and I have nothing in common at all. All I have left of him are stories. Lots of stories, but the plots keep changing without the ending being altered.

She may have told Jerald and Jessica a different story, but I doubt it. My brother's stories involving our mother, in general, are filled with a pulsating atypical flare. They all end with an applause, head nods and machoistic daps that echo his friends' cemented approval. I think she leaned onto Jerald's personality type more than she did mine because, unlike mine, his eyes were unjudging and never expected much of her. She was his mom, and that was good enough for him: a parental title, a family member, and another capital *J*. My sister's stories are not much different, but they are told with a more careful construct. She adored our mother for reasons that never made much sense to me. I never bothered to duct tape her broken memories or fill in holes. In a way, I sometimes enjoyed her refreshing take. Her memories of our mother sounded motherly and bordered a duality of sanity and fairy tale. She granted her a sampling of decently measured kindness, which made us appear to be under the guidance of a very good parent. A parent I secretly wished she was, but one I rarely ever encountered.

"I remember when Mommy used to..." she would blurt out with a smile, transitioning into a semi-poetic epilogue about something our mother did, or said, when Jessica was a little girl. She was quiet as a child, as if she was saving her loudness for these aforementioned parenting fables. An epilogue—that's what it felt like. A farewell, an adieu to a story, or chapter, that undoubtedly was littered with inexplicable gaps. She would smile and proudly show off how wonderful our mother was. She painted her canvas with heart-filled final chapters, completely avoiding the utter disdain our mom had for being "a mom" at times. Joyce wasn't a bad woman; she just wasn't a good mother when we were younger. It feels awkward typing this out, but it feels wrong to keep it in. When I was a kid, I couldn't quite put my finger on why I felt a certain way about her parenting approaches, or how poorly she went about preparing us for life. However, time and grace have cursed me with an altered view. I no longer see her as a faded childhood misunderstanding, but rather as a woman who misunderstood my childhood. Her love life created a sizeable rift between she and I, making it difficult to accept of any love she had for my life. And to this day, I find it hard to tell her love story accurately because, for one, she didn't tell me much and, secondly, I'm afraid to discover that most of it was a lie.

She loved men. Not "love, love", nor the romantic fuzzy, heart in your throat, lips get dried, love. Naw, Poochie (her childhood nickname I learned later in life) loved having a man. Any man. My grandmother, her mom, said it was because my grandfather died when my mother was a little girl. If she never recovered, then having a man was some type of answer to a question that died when she was seven. Present fathers and good dads are built like romanticized giants when you're that age. They are childhood behemoths that hold superhuman powers in the same hands that can hide strawberry taffies without squishing them. They are both real and mythical, lovable and fearful, all at once, with arms built for swinging and shoulders that can carry you away from the absoluteness of gravity. Goliaths in a rose garden, catering to flowers just learning how to bloom. While other little girls were busy asking for rain, Joyce was still stumbling from the loss of a father, as well as a first gardener. I used to tell myself I would one day ask her why she "loved" so many men and why she brought so many of them around us. As I got older, though, I kind of stopped caring. Yet, when I became a dad myself, a giant in my daughters' gardens of love, some of it also started to make sense. They were old wounds, however, and wounds should be picked at when they were scabs—not scars.

Saturdays were filled with my siblings and I cleaning up while Shirley Murdock's "As We Lay", and Vesta Williams' "Congratulations", kept our mother entranced in an offbeat tone. Her voice trembling to maintain its pitch, her eyes trying to convey the relatability of it all to her three-person-audience. We would smile and repeated the words, playing our dual parts as both back-up singers and concertgoers. The tickets were cheap, so we regularly attended. All we were asked to pay was our attention, and our mother's winks were our silent promises that we could keep the change. I liked when she was like this, singing, in a happy state. If felt forced at times, but force meant movement, action. It meant something was getting done and it was a welcomed mood compared to the opposite. Her sad states were always quiet, so we stayed in whatever counties or cities we called our bedrooms at the time. Kids aren't supposed to make noise when things are silent. I was never quite sure why, but I always made certain my whispers never broke the rules. Saturdays, however, were not quiet days. Those days were for living room amateur R&B performances at our mother's "happy" state fairs, and we were cordially invited.

Our record player was dusty but still nice, a Rent-A-Center piece. I think we owed money on it; however, it had so many roaches in it they probably didn't want us to bring it back. It always traveled with us whenever we moved. I blamed it for our insect friends always tagging along, but then again, the couches had roaches too, so it bearing all the blame wasn't fair. I never touched it, never learned how to play it. Rule number whatever my mother blurted out at the time: *You never touch a person's record player* (or radio, or anything playing music for that matter). Black cultural concessions like these were easily appreciated and universally accepted. A black person's music was their voice, but a black woman's music was her soul. Joyce's music connected her to a flood of memories and ideas. Some were lived experiences, and some existed only in her mirage of what love was supposed to feel like. She and that record player often stood under the pergola of her imagination, the two of them intangibly and harmonically engaged to a figment. She was always singing, and it was always playing songs, love songs.

Not "lovely" songs, but ones that carried a rehashed circular message. Someone was sleeping with someone's man, or some guy was with some woman he shouldn't have been with. No one was ever caught cheating in these songs. Just two people serenading indefensible excuses for their defenseless infidelities over music for three or four minutes, until the song reduced to a few vinyl scratches. My mother was always singing them, playing them. It was like she was talking to herself about herself. I never knew which woman my mother was in these "love songs" because I didn't know anything about her men. They were always just there. Sometimes jobless, always drunk. Neither of them lived a life I wished to mirror, but I would always look at them and be afraid of my fate. Is this it? Is this who I will become? Woman beater? Womanizer? A non-bill-payer? A drunken ex-con? A brok—

"Jimmy!" my mom yelled from down the hall.

"Yes, ma'am?" I replied, leaving my last thought on pause.

"Go get my sheets from the clothesline outside."

"Okay."

The Yellow house we lived in on 7th Terrace didn't have any washer/dryer hookups. If they did, we never had appliances to hook them up to. We washed clothes at the laundromat and quickly garbage bagged them up and hurried home. Living in Florida provided the perfect excuse to not waste quarters on the dryers. Nearly every house or apartment had a clothesline outside, two large metal structures that looked like the letter *T*. They stood about twenty feet apart, attached to each other with a thick line of string you would pin your wet clothes on to dry. You could tell when the houses, or apartments, were empty because the empty ones didn't have strings connecting the *Ts*. That was our clue, as kids, that we could sneak into a particular yard. We'd hop the fence to steal mangoes to die for, lemons we never trusted, and oranges that mirrored the ones on state license plates in front of white vans parked down streets that cops pretended they didn't own. A few times, people still lived there, but we were too quick to get caught and too naïve to truly care. I laughed to myself while taking the sheets down and draping them across my arms.

"Clothesline outside," I mockingly repeated.

How can clothesline be anywhere other than outside? Why did she tell me to go outside? I knew where the clotheslines were at; even if I didn't know, I knew they were not... inside. I kept this little, sly-ass conversation to myself. I replayed it in my head as I closed the back door and headed to her room down the hall on the right. Carrying the sheets, I noticed they smelled nice, like fancy nice. We didn't have fancy things, but our outside clothes had nice smells that lasted long enough to at least convince myself that they were clean. I made sure I shook them out really well before I came in to avoid bringing new resident bugs into the house. *Who needs outside roaches mixing with inside roaches?* I would think. My mom didn't say thanks; she was on the phone and just pointed to the bed. I dumped them on her stained mattress, on top of a pile of clothes that were on top of another pile of clothes. Under the heap, I noticed a teal t-shirt that was airbrushed with purple and blue cursive lettering. I quickly grabbed it and was nosily trying to see what it said. My mom was so occupied with her own voice that she didn't notice me at first. As I held up the shirt, I couldn't make out all the words.

"Ulysss? Who is Ulysss?" I mumbled, thinking my mother spelled 'Uselessly' incorrectly.

"Put that down and get outta my damn room!!" she belted, pointing toward the door.

I hurriedly dropped the shirt and left. Still curious about the misspelling and why she was so mad, I slowed as I reached the end of the hall and turned around. The door slammed shut, stealing the light it casted against the wall. I could still feel the coldness of her voice pinching me back to the reality of how hot our house really was that day. Standing in the living room, I was trying to figure out where my brother and sister were. I could hear them outside, but the house wasn't clean. Ugh. *She's already mad*, I whispered. If she came into the living room and realized that her kids left it as junky as her mattress was, she would forget just how junky her mattress was. Then it would commence. More yelling. More saturated convos about how we don't appreciate anything she does. More frustration echoed as love being stitched into the seams of our rear ends from belts losing their stitching. More heat from her voice, adding to the heat that was already crowding the room. *Nah.*

"Jerald! Jessica!" I yelled from the front screen door.

Their joy resonated down the street, playfully. I wasn't going to go look for them, so I yelled again. Standing there, I ran my nails down the small squares on the screen door. My fingertips captured the cadence of the sound they made while sliding across the tiny geometrical boxes, each obeying laws of straightness in a neighborhood where laws were readily broken. I wondered if anyone could see me leaning against it. I scrapped years of crust off the screen with my index finger, blanketing the annoying noise it was beginning to make with thoughts of nothingness. My nose was pressed against its mirrored looseness. There was a little hole right above the screen door handle, covered with tape. Flies would come through it, but they never left out the same way. I continued to pick at it while I was standing there, thinking of nothing, but not willing to move and do more work in the house until my siblings were back.

I wanted to be the "big kid" and just do it myself, but I was always the "big kid" (by default) and that title was tiring. *No one thanks you for carrying their weight around here,* I thought. They just leave more weight for you to carry. It's survival of the fittest but worse. Instead of doing just enough to get by, a small number of people in my neighborhood wanted you to get by for them. Disability checks for people who came over to my house and could miraculously move from wheelchairs when they won bets playing games of Spades. Rich dope dealers asking their babies' mothers for their food stamps and income tax checks. Neighbors asking to borrow sugar because they didn't want to use their own. Hustlers. Con artists. Pimps. Panhandlers. Fathers who didn't visit on weekdays. Mothers who didn't cook on weekends. Little siblings who didn't clean because they knew the oldest child was going to *get a beating* as well—for it all not being completed. Why not wait until survival chores induced fears of not surviving for all the kids? Get other people to do your work for you. That was the game, I was used to it, but wasn't up for playing it that day.

As I called for them again, it sounded like their voices were fading, fruitlessly trying to escape a fate I was certain would arrive shortly if the chores were not completed. I was getting upset because I knew they were aware that shared trouble was arriving along with their late arrival. Opening the door, I heard my name from behind as I was about to step outside.

"Jimmy..." my mother said

"Huh?" I replied, trying to stop my momentum from carrying me toward the yard.

"Don't huh me, boy."

Turning around to correct my choice of words, I was startled by the bright purple words sprawled across my mother's chest. I could finally see the spelling, almost blending into a teal sea. The words were surrounded with small hearts and had "& Joyce" at the bottom.

"I'm about to go to Nisha house for bit. Where yo' brother and sister at?"

"Huh?"

"*Huh* me one more damn time."

"Umm, I'm sorry. I... I don't know. I was trying to find them," I stated while trying not to awkwardly stay transfixed at the new word being stretched out by my mother's large chest.

"Well, you ain't gon find'em standing in da doh. Y'all stay in the house until I get back."

"Yes, ma'am," I replied thinking, *Who is y'all? I don't even know where the rest of "y'all" is even at.*

She got into her little white Toyota, which was built for a woman half her size. The car tilted a bit when she sat inside. I smiled slightly behind the screen door, finger no longer playing with the little hole. I watched as her driver-side tires stared at me and took a deep breath before doing their designated jobs. Rolling the window down, she told me to fold the clothes on her bed. I knew she was going to say it before she said it, but hearing her say it still irritated me. She sped off down the street, beyond the trees in the neighbor's yard that hovered over the sidewalk to the left of where our yard ended. The sun was fading with its usual pre-evening sigh, telling Florida it was tired—although none of us Floridians really cared about how hard it was working. As she drove away, I could hear "Ma! Momma!" coming into clarity on my right. I didn't look to catch up with the voices; I kept staring at the trees. They didn't have mangoes, or license plate oranges, but they were large and old—too old for this neighborhood. My brother interrupted my moment with panting and questions about where our mom was going.

"Where momma went?" he forced out between breaths, my sister following suit.

"I don't know."

"She didn't tell you?"

"Yeah, but I don't remember."

"How you don't remember? She just left..." he puzzled.

"I just don't. She said stay in the house."

I stood in the door as they came in, making sure I didn't lock the screen door with the tape in the corner. I locked the other door and turned the porch light on; unsure when my mother would return. My brother went straight to the kitchen—no hand washing—for leftovers; my sister tacitly disappeared into her bedroom. I sat on the couch and pushed my head back against the worn-out cushioning, adjusting to avoid the coarse ridges from old scratches tickling the nape of my neck. Drowning out the sound of the microwaved pulsations, I whispered to myself, "Ulysses. Who is Ulysses?"

4

room number.

What's in a name? I remember patients' faces and causes of death, but not many of their names. When we are born most of our parents rack their brains trying to find the right label to give us, the perfect moniker. Throughout life we are identified and personalized through memorized channels that our names tunnel for us inside worlds we create for ourselves. Sometimes consciously, sometimes by happenstance—either/or, the end result is an evoked idea of "who we are," which we feel provides us with meaning. For instance, I am Jimmy Moss. Some people hear those words and smile; some don't feel anything at all. I feel something though, a connection, something of value. I have looked into mirrors and uttered supportive phrases around my name, and, in doing so, have been able to un-tunnel myself out of some dark places and dead-end roads. We all have. We all should be proud, that is, when our names are called to step up and become a champion of something great and monumental. And even if that moment never comes, I feel like we should at least be attentive enough to know when it occurs for others. It's often heralded by their name being called, a salutation, or an introduction. "Hello, I am such and such," then a smile. The expectations are that of a positive epithet; yet, that is all involuntarily lost when you get admitted to a hospital. You're no longer a name; HIPPA won't allow us to "talk about you," so, reflexively, you become a number. A room number.

That's often how you're remembered in the end. Mr.-or-Mrs. "*Wutsaname? Remember, the patient in room 423... last month?*", followed by agreement, finger snapping, and head nods. A story is usually told. Someone may vaguely remember your name, but most of the time they don't. They remember why you were admitted, the extremes surrounding your hospital stay, quite possibly how and when you died (as if it matters to you at that point), and, inevitably, your room number. The pride your family will take in ensuring that your name is spelled correctly in off-white obituary booklets is not shared by hospital staff. It's not that we don't care, but rather we don't remember every James, Susan, or Tom—just their numbers. Lab values. Blood pressure readings and fever zeniths. Small things stand out like, "Remember his Cr was 22!?" or "Yeah, her hemoglobin was 2.1." These critically distinct outliers will become memorialized by those who will care for you in the end and hold your hand when you take your last breath. We can recall some patients, the frequent fliers and chronic vent patients. They spend more time with us than they do with their families, but those are the exceptions. Their names being remembered reflects their disease states. We recollect their various illnesses, and their identities merely provide a convenient framework we use to tell the story behind their suffering.

If you've worked in healthcare for any fraction of your life, then you have tightly woven memories about a lot of rooms. It's almost like a superstitious façade we enjoy keeping afloat. More patients die more often in specific sections of your little work arena. It's a thing, like black clouds surrounding some coworkers or the ill-effects of full moons on ER and ICU visits. No dark magic, just stories. Countless stories. I never fully appreciated how sensitive these beliefs were until I started blowing them off. Consequently, I started getting my ass handed back to me during crazy full-moon shifts. Even worse, it seemed like the pairing of particular charge nurse teammates and me somehow yielded higher admission (and death) rates.

"Moss, it's you and me tonight? It's gonna be a shitshow. Ugh," Linda blurted at me, followed by a fist dap and a smile.

She wasn't lying. Room 205 was empty and sound asleep when our night shift started. A few hours later, though, it was wide awake, rousing up, only to find itself empty and dark. Oblivious to this unearthing of bad humors, I was in my call room, Netflixing (but not chillin'). The landline phone rang, violently making it known that my services or expertise were needed. Not every call I get at work is an emergency, but no call is ever made to "see how everything is going." I jumped up to answer it. I wasn't asleep; hell, I rarely "sleep at work," but I often lie down to rest my eyelids. For some reason, nurses think the room is plush and sleep-worthy, but it's hard to find any comfort in a twin bed, with a green fire-resistant covering.

"Hey, Boss, they need you in the CDU," a voice quickly delivered over the phone. *Click.*

I grabbed my P-100 mask, my face shield, tossed the apple I was eating into the trash, and headed downstairs to the CDU. The CDU is a Clinical Decision Unit; observation and chest pain patients are usually housed there. The aim is to avoid unnecessary hospital admissions for patients who are acutely sick but not deathly ill. During the pandemic, however, our hospital (well, almost every hospital) was no longer afforded the luxury of reserving convenient spaces for patients who were sick but not *that sick*. We transformed it into a COVID low acuity admission area, hoping to limit the transmission of the disease to other patrons and staff members. It was equipped with windows facing the backside parking lot. Since it was on the first floor, family members could come up to the windows and see their loved ones. They would bring pets, healing energy, and offer more loving cures than the medicinal ones we were scrambling to find. It was a humanistic reprieve; patients and family members loved it, staff members wished we had more of it.

"Hey, Linda, they called me about this COVID patient in the CDU, how many rooms we got?" I asked over my cellphone as I headed down the hall toward the elevator, broad steps with a slightly urgent pace. I never run to emergencies because one time I fell and almost became "the emergency."

"One and a code bed. If you take this patient, she will go into 205," Linda replied.

"Cool."

Shuffling around the corner, I eagerly pushed the elevator down button, hoping I'd get lucky and hear a *bing*. No *bing*. Rolling my eyes, I mumbled to myself to stop being lazy and take the stairs—it's two flights. As soon as I entered the stairwell, I heard a soft *bing* as the door closed behind me. Of course. Trying to not think about what was possibly awaiting my arrival down the hall, I refocused my attention on my wasted apple in my call room. I could have saved it, but this is a COVID room—even if she doesn't come to the ICU, that apple will be browner than me when I returned. You don't walk into COVID rooms for "a few minutes"; it becomes an event. PPE. Masks that barely fit. That lingering fear that all the wiping and hand sanitizing in the world won't stop one little virus from invading the crevices of your body and wreaking havoc.

Even more, I can usually sniff out an ill patient with my sick-dar from the room's door; but these patients required more time, more finesse. Their disease process was so novel that peripheral complications invited themselves without formally announcing their intentions to bring 'harm' along as a guest. I was going to be in that room for a while, so that apple was as good as gone. It was a silly mental retreat, but I love apples. Big apples. Small apples. All apples, except the bitter ones disguised with names that falsely invite the anticipation of sweetness. My favorite kind? Envy apples, from New Zealand. Absolutely the best. It's ironic because the saying goes: An apple a day, keeps the doctor away—yet, I was more than present that evening.

This patient in CDU 7 and I met in the most awkward of ways, but these random hospital meetings are my norm as an ICU attending. I take care of people during their most vulnerable moments, when sickness becomes more than an enemy, and when liveliness is no longer a friend. Most individuals name death as their biggest fear in life; however, that is because they ignore the unassuming inconveniences of *dying*. Senescence. Biological aging. It becomes a parable of sorts, a broken analogy filled with varying characters and plots. Our efforts, as we senesce, are to avoid the finality of death, but we often ignore the devil in the details of dying. We sign contracts each morning with life, signaling, "Yes, we are dying... moving closer to the end of our time here on Earth, but we are okay with it." However, when that moment arrives, when death rises to collect on its pledged settlements, we timidly raise our hands, afraid to say, "Present," since doing so will anchor the truth that (soon) we will no longer be here anymore.

Our contractual naivete offers us an applause each morning, a forgiving tone that fades as soon as we venture out into whatever awaits us in the coming hours. Work. Love. Bills. Burnt toast and kids slowly finishing breakfast cereal. Pets that follow their instincts to only follow us in fractions. Paychecks we've already spent before they are deposited into our accounts. Upcoming vacations. Weddings. Weight we are reminded to lose, juxtaposed against arguments we vainly put forth efforts to win. The joys and pains, all balanced into memories we fashion into photo collages online, await nervously for outside approval via heart-shaped likes and shares. We live tirelessly until illness and tragedy steal away whatever energy reserves we, somehow, embarrassingly forgot to inventory. We try to ignore that death is inevitable. However, the process of dying reminds us it has never forgotten our signatures we forfeited many moons ago. It still remembers when we traded the beckoning silence of moonlight for the chance to exchange our fading darkness for more light under the sun. And when death and dying signal to us that they are overlapping mirrors of coldness, that's when they call me.

I got "that" call, my second one about the patient in CDU 7, as I was heading toward her room, on Thanksgiving morning, around 1 a.m. Dr. Kondowe, a Hospitalist and one of my frequent partners during the evening shift, is usually very chill and hardly rattled, but I could hear something different in her voice.

"Moss, this lady is sick."

She goes on to tell me all of her current hospital problems—COVID-19 viral infection, acute hypoxic respiratory failure, multifocal pneumonia, NSTEMI (a minor heart attack), bilateral pulmonary embolisms (clots in her lungs), to name a few. Each signifying severe complications of her viral inflammation and the escalating cytokine storm brewing inside of her body, which she is oblivious to in any fashion. Bad stuff. Super bad stuff. Her clock is ticking, understandably, but the interplay of anxiety shared by a physician and their patient is a special occurrence. When a practitioner is urgently concerned about their patient, there is a universal seriousness in their tone. Their voice inflections almost dare you to question their clinical gestalt, but also passionately invite you to listen. This is "their patient," with whom they have established a binding pact. It is equally a social and professional agreement, with an understood silently legal tenor, where governing roles have been identified and trust has been earned. A patient's trust is invaluable. You can have as many diplomas as letters behind your name scattered across a wall of superiority, but if they don't trust you, well, save the paper on your prescription pad—they will not comply with your recommendations. Thus, the responsibility of being an inflexible and stout representative for a patient becomes both an evoked liability and an honor. In the face of illness, you are not only their voice, you are also their hope. I could hear that hope resonating in Dr. Kondowe's voice. She wasn't calling me for pleasantries; her patient was sick.

At admission, she was started on standard COVID-19 therapy, as well as blood thinners, and she was slowly starting to recover. Nine days in the hospital, and before Dr. Kondowe called me, she was slated to go home. Big apples. Unfortunately, she had an acute complication: she was bleeding into her abdomen. Quickly. Drastically. Her blood pressure was dropping, and her kidneys were shutting down, noted by the lack of urine in her foley catheter, despite the few liters of IV fluids she recently received. More importantly, her respiratory status was worsening—she went from only requiring a little amount of oxygen to needing 100% oxygen via CPAP in a matter of hours. As Dr. Kondowe was updating me outside of her room, I stared at the patient via the thin lower-case-L-shaped glass window in the door. The CPAP mask covered her entire face; her shoulders slanted forward, tripoding, in an effort to stent open her lungs. Her torso was wide but tiny, partially hidden underneath a large hospital gown. However, even from afar I could tell she was working hard to breathe. She was expending whatever reserves she had to avoid relinquishing her failing grasp on a task that, up to a few hours ago, she had absolutely under control: breathing. Autopilot was no longer an option. She had the flight controls in her sweat-drenched and tremulous palms. Visibly shaken, she was fighting to keep the people outside of her small alphabetical shaped window from bringing in more bad news about what was noticeably occurring inside of her room.

Not wanting to waste any time further assessing her in the CDU, I quickly moved her to the ICU. If there were going to be any immediate emergencies, I wanted to ensure she was in my arena, with my team in attendance and with my tools readily available. Before speaking with her, I scanned her chart more intently. Everything Dr. Kondowe told me over the phone was starting to look a lot worse on paper. Her kidneys were not failing, they failed. She was not anemic; she was actively hemorrhaging. I remember thinking, *She's dying... Shit.*

But then something in her medical history jumped out at me: breast cancer. She was actively fighting it. Beating it. Surviving it. This wasn't just any run-of-the-mill patient, fighting a debilitating viral respiratory infection. This was someone battling one of the most dreaded and deadliest diseases modern women courageously face: breast cancer-- and she was kicking its ass. Yet, here she was, in distress, on 100% oxygen, fighting for her life, possibly aware of what stood in front of her, but most likely unsure of its distance. Normalcy felt further away than it did the morning before, as the conversation flipped from her potentially being discharged to being rapidly transferred to the ICU.

What happened?

What was missed?

Was it something overlooked or unexpected?

What if she was home when this occurred?

Was it COVID-related?

Things were improving... right?

I imagined these thoughts, and many more, raced across her mind as her stretcher pierced the veil of another floor's fog of sick COVID anomalies. She was heading to an area where "the experts" assumed control of all planes fated to crash; however, their patients were all "still" dying despite their expertise. Monitors were attached to more wires that were eventually attached to her. Her aliveness was measured in sounds and primary colors oscillating on a screen that faced a door with the lower-case-L-shaped window exchanged for one made entirely of glass. Staring at her, donning my PPE, I wondered how much time

I had to try and convince her to extend her remaining portion of "hope" to me—that is, if she had any hope left to give.

Small in stature, and emotionally calmer than I expected, she was sitting up in bed with her eyes glazed and her focus shattered. Her initial appearance of steadiness was actually multifactorial shock and the placidity of fear settling in. She knew she was ill; her nauseating pain and struggle to breathe echoed those sentiments. I pulled up a chair next to her, introduced myself and tried to explain the very complex series of medical catastrophes currently raging war for "cause of death" in her body. I asked if she understood and her reply gave me a glimpse into her spirit, a view that simply scanning her chart never would have afforded me:

"It's that bad, Doc? Damn. That sucks", followed by a chuckle.

I tried to readdress my wording. Sometimes, how you relay a series of facts can make them understandable. Equally, oversimplifying them can also make patients question their decision to freely entrust their hope into your care. Organ by organ, I spoke in laymen terms, trying to clarify what I said moments early, while she still was trying to get situated into her new environment. New nurses. New bed. New wall paintings matching the off-peach décor of the room. The large visitor's parking lot window was gone. It was replaced with a view of the hallway outside her glass door, now crowded with ICU personnel streaming about like department store passersby in front of discounted sections they've already looked over. I spoke more slowly, more intently, aiming to invoke some sense of confidence and possibly some relief. Her eyes left mine and stared ahead. Tearfully, she asked me, "Okay, so what now?"

I paused, grabbed her hand, leaned in closer and told her, "Well... now, you do what you've been doing before you got here: you fight. We fight. Your nurses and the team are right here with you. Let me worry about the bad stuff, you focus on the good... and we fight. I'm going to have to put a breathing tube inside of your lungs because your breathing mechanics are worsening, and you are beginning to tire. But you won't feel or remember a thing. I promise you that you will be comfortable, and you will be in good hands. You will be fully asleep, something like a medically induced coma, to ensure you aren't in any pain or distress. I have started you on multiple medications to keep your blood pressure up, and you need more blood products as well. And because your kidneys are not working at the moment you will need twenty-four-hour dialysis so I need to put in a dialysis catheter... but none of this stuff will work if you are not willing to fight... I need you to fight. Your family will fight and they need you to fight too. If we are going to beat this, if you are going to get better, it will only happen if you are leading the way."

Nodding her head assuredly, eyes drowning in fearful tears, her voice muffled behind a large, smothering CPAP mask that still nearly covered her entire face, she boldly stated: "Let's do this."

And she did. Ten days later, off dialysis, breathing tube removed. After suffering one of her most daunting crises as an adult, she was making baby steps toward recovery followed by more baby steps toward herself again. I was absent while all of this was occurring, busy at other hospitals working long hours, having my confidence shaken by death after death. On my first day back at the hospital she was admitted to, the first thing I asked was, "How's the patient in 205 doing?" I spoke in present tense, as if my tone and careful choice of words was some type of buoyant request offered to random, inwardly vague, invisible gatekeepers of fate.

"She's doing well. She's actually downstairs... about to be discharged," the ICU Secretary stated with a smile. "We've been following her chart from afar! Isn't that wonderful?"

Discharged. A smile flushed over my face, as I rushed down to her floor, hurriedly trying to catch her before she went home. After donning my attire, I walked in and saw her sitting on the side of the bed. Quiet in thought, anxious to leave, she was wearing a large, navy-blue hoodie, with the hood bundled up against the back of her head, and pajama pants. She was scrolling through her cellphone, oblivious to the nasal cannula prong residing on top of her left nare. Seeing my face after I knocked on her door, she smiled and waved me in, inviting me to sit down, and we talked. I told her how happy I was about her outcome and that she was on my mind the entire time I was away. She stated that she remembered me and our talk, but apologized for not remembering all the details. I explained that she was in a medically induced coma, to which she laughed and said, "Oh, those were some good drugs, Doc. I haven't had dreams like that since the 70s." She laughed some more.

And that's what the two of us did, sat there, laughing out loud, followed by joyful tears and a warm hug. I asked if I could share her story online (she agreed) because there were nurses, doctors, techs, RTs and pharmacists all over the world who needed to hear of her victory, who needed to be reminded why we "go so hard" despite the failures and losses, despite the agony of so many defeats. We fight because deep inside, behind the shadows of doubt and under the flatlines of disbelief, something inside of each of us still hopes for patients like her. We want our patients to survive, to postpone death. We want their last days to NOT be in hospitals or to be clouded with suffering or having suffering prolonged. The escape for us is that when we are given someone's hope, it becomes a reminder that hope still matters and exists.

The irony of it all, though, is that deep inside we are still aware that it is all just a brief pause on an extended warranty. Death is coming, as Virgil once noted, and it twitches our ear. How we respond to this memento is so varied and so individualized that it is hard to convey whether a particular response is appropriate or not. A person's approach to recognizing the overlapping of death and dying is rarely shared or discussed; often there is no time to even consider the process. Yet, when it occurs, and medical staff members are witnesses to such an occurrence, it offers us a chance to become a part of a patient's efforts of temporarily removing death from the equation. My patient was able to leave the hospital and spend a few more months with her family members. Unfortunately, I was later told, she succumbed to the gravity of residual scars left on her physical form. Breast cancer and post-COVID syndromes, along with kidney failure and blood clots, were all calculated enemies of time, awaiting their turn to voice their unwillingness to leave from their respective podiums until they were heard. We gave her back an extended version of the nervous hope she extended us months before her passing, and something tells me she enjoyed every minute of it.

A few more months. A few more weeks, days, or hours. Whatever it means to be and to feel alive has value. It is not always tangible, but it most certainly is very real. The details are often blurred and vaguely recalled, but the impression it leaves on us, as medical professionals, is not lost. We carry their stories in our smiles, share their sadness in our tears. They give us a part of themselves, their most vulnerable parts, and in return we offer them our best efforts and our compassion in the form of privacy-laced remembrances. The patients we represent are with us—in both spirit and memory—albeit, sometimes, only via lab values or a particular room down the hall, like Room 205.

Yeah. I'm never going to forget her room number. More importantly, I am also never going to forget her name: Pam.

primary colors.

M ost of my childhood was a series of colors. Primary colors. Off-shade colors; pastels and divided rainbows. We searched for the gold at the end with a blinded excitement, yet only found more reasons to not believe in the magic behind rainbows anymore. But there was always a color. I remember specific moments based on what color house we lived in. My dad breaking into our home and leaving death threats: The Yellow house, Fort Lauderdale. My mom skipping town with her new boyfriend, taking Jessica and leaving Jerald and me behind: The Brown townhouse, North Lauderdale. Getting babysat by T Man, while he cooked us the only food we had in the house (flour and water—he called it pancakes, but it was just flour and water): The Gray apartments, Collier City. Last time I can remember living with my father: That was in a small Blue house, in a new development they tried to pretend wasn't the projects, but since it was built for (and filled with) people from the projects it was still the projects. Pompano Beach, down the street from Nisha.

My mom and Nisha were best friends, I think. The way my mom told it: Nisha used to like Ulysses for a bit, but then he went to jail. Poochie probably made this story up, but Joyce was the one who told me. I don't know how much of (most of) what Joyce told me was true or a beautiful lie, but it's the only truth I was told when Joyce was being a mom. After the death threat my dad left us in the Yellow house, Nisha told my mom that she "knew a guy"—a bad guy. He used to fight people for drugs back in the day, but once he got "clean" he liked fighting so much that he did it just to make money. My mom found out he was getting out of jail soon and went to go see him. She wanted to hire him to beat up my dad before anyone else hired him (work was plentiful). Whatever happens when you meet a guy who is in jail and start liking him to the point that he becomes your boyfriend must have happened, because that's what happened. Next thing you know, I found his name on a teal t-shirt on my mom's laundry pile covered mattress, back when we lived in the Yellow house—noted above.

Ulysses was medium brown skin toned and tall, but I was a small boy when I first met him, so his height was probably an illusion. He had sharp cheek bones and was built like someone copied his upper body from a He-Man doll. He wasn't bowlegged, like my dad, but his legs were thin and still chiseled. He had a narrow stance when he walked and a wide smile whenever he lied. He mostly wore silk V-necks t-shirts and straight-legged jeans with creases that looked like they were factory installed. His hands were calloused and thin, fingertips darker than his palms, fingernails sharper than his wit. He kept a low fade, with tight waves, and was always brushing his head when he wasn't talking. And since he didn't say much, he was always brushing his head.

Monday through Friday he was a different human: calm, sober and even nice to us at times. He cut grass with a local commercial lawn crew filled with black and Hispanic guys but ran by white guys. They all traded laughter for frowns every morning during roundup time, and instantly traded it all back in as the clock moved closer to the evening. I can't remember the company's name. I only remember the stale green, long-sleeve shirts they wore that smelled so much like warm summer grass, that looking at his work clothes in the laundry basket always tightened my skin into an itch. Their pants were a deep forest green; the crew all wore matching shades and brown gloves. It looked like they were dressed for winter, although Florida's winters still felt like summer—so there's that. I liked Ulysses during the week. We didn't bother him, and he didn't bother us. We were "Joyce's kids," not his, and he regularly reminded us. I think he had a daughter, about my age, but I can't recall any collegial weekends of her visiting us, which was smart. Ulysses was a different human on the weekends, far different than the human he was when he was working.

I would come home from school Friday afternoons, drop off my bag, and hit the streets with my friends. As the sunlight turned to streetlights, I'd hurry home for dinner, and he would be lifting weights and drinking in the driveway with his friends. Big weights. I was in awe with how the bar would bend every time he lifted it off the rack. Hundreds of pounds, bouncing off his chest, while his friends intoxicatingly urged him on. Sweat spilling to the ground underneath the bench, every vein in his arms, begging to be stared at and coldly demonstrating how much more powerful he was compared to the so called "little man" of the house: me. Weights and high fives were exchanged for the remote control and more beers. He watched a lot of sports; I think the first time I watched a basketball game was with him and his friend, Red.

Red lived across town, in Plantation. He worked for the city, so he had "a good job." We never met his kids either, but Ulysses always joked that he had a "lot of'em". Red was a big guy, but more fat than muscle. His freckles disappeared when he smiled, but his smile never seemed to lie like Ulysses' did. I would stare at his work boots and try to guess their size, 12s, 13s, maybe larger. I used to wonder if my feet would get that big or if they would stay small like my mom said my dad's feet were. But I didn't want my dad's feet, I wanted big feet like Red's. He walked big and stood with a confidence that radiated: No Fear. He wasn't afraid of Ulysses like I (or my mom) was, and I liked that. I think they did time in prison together; I'm not sure. Poochie once said something about it on the phone with a friend of hers, yet Joyce never told me in person. Red talked with his hands, and he never finished a story because he would start chuckling so hard that it always ended too early. Most of the jokes were over my head, though. They would argue over monies not paid from bets they barely remembered. The liquor had them in a buzzed mixture of steely-eyed anger and bullshitting laughter that typically induced man hugs. Yeah, I liked Red. He kept Weekend Ulysses in check, and off my mother's face. They never fought when Red was around, but when he wasn't visiting, they argued like Red was a roommate that bailed on them for the rent. Those weekends sucked. No TV. No sports. No games. No imaginary stepsister to keep her dad's drunken anger at bay. Just beer and no Red.

Red-less weekends all started the same: us kids outside and Ulysses on the couch, hogging the remote. My mother would usually stay out of his way until he found a reason to blame her for being in it. His Old Milwaukee forty-ounce bottles cluttered the broken, brown coffee table that never saw a coffee cup a day in its life. Sometimes, he would let me watch a few shows with him, but I think he mostly just forgot I was in the room. Watching TV with Ulysses was also the first time I ever saw a pornographic film. He was up drinking late one night and fell asleep with the VCR on. I woke up in the middle of the night and went into the living room. I saw, what looked like someone urinating on a naked female, and was in as much shock as a nine-year-old boy would probably be in that moment. Curious, I hit rewind when it went off, but he woke up and kicked me from his seat on the couch.

"TAKE your lil ass to bed!" he growled as his foot steamed in the side of my hip.

This was at the Green house, in Lauderhill (a small city, west of Fort Lauderdale). We moved into the Green house after we left the Yellow house on 7th Terrace. In response to receiving the aforementioned death threat, Poochie had planned to hire Ulysses to beat my dad up, but since they were dating at this point, he did it for free. They also got married at the Green house, right in the front yard. I remember the weddings photos next to the faux stonework on the outside that didn't match the shoddy craftsmanship on the inside. It was the same house my grandmother would walk through and pray for God to protect her grandbabies. The same house my dad sent goons to seeking revenge for what Ulysses did to his chest. The same house at which, just a few months after their wedding, an intoxicated Ulysses would beat my mother in while she was in the corner bleeding from her face- lifeless, but not dead.

I liked that house, but I liked the Yellow house more. They both were quite close to each other, both still in the hood—i.e., on opposite sides of I-95. This interstate highway divided the city, as well as other cities like Miami and Pompano, into east and west residential rivalries no one openly spoke of. Poor people lived west of I-95; rich people lived east of it, closer to the beaches. If you were driving through south Florida back in the 80s, you defined your neighborhood by whatever street name that signaled the exit you got off. Sunrise. Oakland. Broward. Those neighborhoods were further divided by income lines that situated Lamborghini dealerships down the street from pawn shops and KFCs. I-95 wasn't that far from the beach; any exit could take you there. You just had to drive through the east side of town where the rich people stayed. When we lived in the Yellow house (it was closer to the west side of the city than it was to the east side of it), and whenever we had a working car, we used to take drives to the beach on weekends. Inexpensive staycations, looking outside of half-opened front and back seat windows that served as both lukewarm air conditioners and front row seats to lifestyles only people east of I-95 could afford.

Near the end of one of the streets that ran into the beach, was an underground walkway tunnel that ran perpendicular to Highway A1A. This long, winding road contoured most of the eastern Florida coast. The tunnel connected the parking lot across the street directly to the summery hot sand granules that always felt like red coals painted the color of light brown gravel. It was poorly lit and always smelled of urine; fresh graffiti paint lined the walls. If you ran fast enough, it felt like you were watching a Sesame Street alphabet movie out of the corner of your eyes. There were small pieces of glass on the ground, but we still ran down it, barefoot and reckless, until we reached the threshold of our mini-Atlantis. Even if you wore sandals, the coal-like sand would still climb over the sides and unabatedly invite themselves into your sensory world of joy. The heat stole away your attention before the cool ocean water bullied it right back. Screaming and listening to our echoes dissipate as they abruptly crashed into the sound of waves dominating the air, we dove into the tide-ripping water with a selfish neglect. During one visit, we also, like other families for once, brought food and drinks. Whoever my mom was dating at the time (before Ulysses) had his beer mixed in with our dollar store juices, sandwiches, and non-waterproof snacks. It was all stuffed into a Styrofoam cooler, which somehow never seemed to keep things cool enough to make sense for it to be in a cooler.

"This sandwich is hot," I'd say, hoping it was loud of enough for my mom to hear me complaining under an unclouded August sun. The heat just made her quicker to snap back.

"You'ont like, you ain't gotta eat it," she'd reply, not looking in my direction.

My brother and sister loved the beach. I think for them it was just another day to play. Their excitement made it easy to forget we were just some poor people going to the beach. No one ever called it a picnic because that would assume the experience was picturesque. Polaroid-like and photogenic. The beach was a good idea, cheap and easy to get to. However, it also forced me to look at all the stuff other people had that I tried to forget that I didn't have. I liked it enough, especially smelling the salt in the air as you got closer and closer to the ocean's unending summons of foamy-tipped waves. Despite the fun parts, I always felt like our trips could have been better planned. Actual blankets to lie on instead of beach towels. Better sandals or flip-flops to traverse the devil's sand. Beach umbrellas like all the white people had. Buckets and small shovels to build sandcastles. More damn ice to keep the sandwiches cool.

We sat out our customary fifteen minutes to let our food digest. The God-fearing complications of going back into the water too early were never clearly outlined. It probably had something to do with God and bread or cramps. Since black people fear God with an unhealthiness equaling untreated cancers, it stood as a good enough reason to not upset my mother with another question. I stilled asked it though, in my head. She, unknowingly, gave me my answer when I asked if it had been fifteen minutes, immediately after a four-minute song finished on our little portable radio, and she said, "Yes." And since God wasn't looking, we quickly ran back into the water.

The drives back to the Yellow house were never very long. My siblings, asleep after trading in their energy for hours of skin darkening dosages of ultraviolet sunlight, were still lighter than me. I stared at them both, innocent and quiet between my brother's snores. I used to use their lighter skin tones as an inward justification that I was adopted or from another family. I loved them, I just felt different. Not better, I guess; just not like them. All siblings are unique in their own way, but mine were more similar to each other than they were like me. I was a few years older than them; they were a year apart. That time gap between us felt like eons before I even knew what an eon was. I felt smarter and more reserved than them, but they looked happier. You could almost trace the joy they had during our childhood without lifting a finger from their smiles. Youthful forgetfulness. It was as if they were completely oblivious to how poor we were. Maybe they did know, but just didn't care as much as I did. I cared though, a lot. I hated being poor; hated being from the hood. I hated living on the west side of I-95, next to winos and liquor stores that never told them no. I hated the smell of arriving at certain parts of towns we lived in; it felt like the sun knew we were poor and tried to spoil things faster. I hated that we nev—

"Who left the light on in my room?" my mom blurted out, interrupting my thought.

As we pulled into the driveway, we gaspingly noticed that the front door was wide open; someone had kicked it in. The screen door was still intact, pretending to hide the obvious. I followed behind my mother and her guy friend. Standing in the living room, I felt the carpet's heaviness (i.e., filthiness) under my bare feet. Quietly and calmly, I gestured to my siblings behind me to remain quiet as well. The rest of the lights started to illuminate the small three-bedroom house. The hallway was filled with movement. My mother's shadow shrunk at the corridor opening as she walked through it, out into the living room, toward the kitchen. Still quiet, my siblings and I waited for our next anticipated command. My mother ignored our patient obedience, grabbed the matching yellow house phone, and called 911.

I didn't want to upset her or make any sudden movements; neither did Jerald or Jessica. We were scared and not even sure why we were scared. Nothing looked different. Everything was in place. My eight-year old detective senses were trying to look for clues; that lasted for all of three minutes when it dawned on me: we're poor as hell. *Who is going to steal from us?* There was nothing of any value in the house, except the extra hour of sleep we occasionally stole on Saturday mornings. The couch pillows were somewhat new, but it was stained from the soda Jerald spilled on them the first day we brought them home. If you stared hard enough, you could also see the tears he shed after getting a beating for his ill-fated accident. The cops arrived, quicker than usual. My mother showed them a piece of paper that she refused to let them hold for themselves at first. I listened as my mother changed her voice's tone and pitch; she sounded like a receptionist. She spoke with a steady pace that only appeared when talking to bill collectors. My wishing she spoke like that more often bothered me a bit. I wondered, *Why didn't she speak like that to us—with respect and concern?* My sister's sniffling interrupted my thought.

"Shhh!" I whispered, hand over my lips while my eyes quickly glanced at my brother, who was staring at the police.

They looked around the house, their cop lights piercing through the front window curtains, leaving cherry and blueberry disco flashes across the faces of any adult who walked by. I took it as a sign they didn't plan on staying long. It was also evident they had no interest in whatever the hell just happened. They didn't even notice the three shirtless, sand-covered kids frozen in the living room, staring at them like ashy black mimes. My mother's guy friend was outside, smoking cigarettes. He seemed unbothered and uninterested in the chaos. Unsurprisingly, that night was the last time I saw him. Quiet guy, stealing all the ice coldness on the beach, now stealing away from my mother's side while she talking to the police. After the cops left, he helped fix the door, and I am not sure where he went after that. I asked my mom if she wanted me to call Grandma.

"No, don't call her... I'll call her tomorrow."

My sister started crying more after the cops left.

"Girl, whatchu crying for??" my mother asked, angrily but concerned.

"I don't want you to go to jail!" she wept.

"I ain't going to no jail," she said. "The cops already left. They're looking for the bad guys. Come here." She reached out to my sister to give her a hug.

I remember thinking: How does she know they were guys? Did they leave a clue in the note she was holding? What if it was women or teenage boys? What if it was someone we knew? I was playing detective without establishing any serious plans of deduction. Just questions. Partially being curious, mostly being nosy- typical me. Still in our beach clothes, we took our turns in the bathroom and got ready for bed. My mother was on the yellow phone, still holding the letter; teary eyed but calmer now. She sat down on the couch, the long phone cord stretched across the living room air like a generic, yellow tight wireline.

My brother kept running back and forth under it, my sister right behind him. I wanted to play too but I kept thinking about the note. *Who wrote it? What was it? What did it say?*

It was folded by now, in her palm, as she sat back on the couch. Smiling and laughing at this point. *She must be talking to Nisha,* I thought. She only laughed like that with Nisha. She got off the phone, put the letter on the table, and told us to go to bed. I wanted to see what it said but was afraid to piss her off. My plan: Get up early and try to sneak and read it before she woke up. The next morning, plan in mind, I skipped the bathroom and made a beeline for the living room. No note. All I could see from the end of the hallway was the spot my mother was last sitting in, next to the pillows covered with soda stains and my brother's barely visible tears.

6

more time.

6 3 years.

The hospital policy says, "No visitors allowed". It's a new policy, objective at best, subjectively enforced. With the nod of a head, or titled eyebrow, exceptions can be made; they should be made. I mean, they have been married for sixty-three years.

In the middle of a pandemic, my team and I felt as if we were on the outside of humanity. The PPE was protective against novel viruses, but it did very little to shield us from human emotions. Phone calls were never brief. My nursing teammates' willingness to field frontline family queries, while juggling care plan charting and administering medications we weren't even sure were working, offered me a few moments of reflection. I often found myself in my office whenever the pace allowed, with my head facing downward, arms resting against my lap. Even when I was in an area that was safe to "breathe," I was still hesitant to do so at times.

Mid-shift, I was told that the family members of the patient at the end of the hall, whose care was becoming futile, were en route. I called her husband (and their son) earlier to come visit her in the afternoon. I didn't want to have a detailed conversation over the phone; we've done that already. Each day we spoke about "the plan for the day", and each day that plan changed. I've tried to stay neutral, firm in my delivery but not too depressing with my words.

However, I think they could hear in my voice what they felt in their hearts: it's time.

Balancing these moments is grounded in the other side of "doctoring" and "nursing." It's etched in calligraphic mission statements lining the halls of various schools we've attended, only to be easily forgotten in the everyday hustle of trying to keep our jobs. Yet it always comes back quickly, that fragmented sense of duty, when needed. Not to all of us, but to many of us. Our humanistic selves borrow the spotlight from the many faces of "I'm okay" we bravely showcase to the world—small winks and beveled smiles.

I tend to internalize whenever mine arrives, ever so careful not to seem stoic. Admittedly, I'm always wondering when the day will come that I will no longer be able to hide my tightened shoulders behind the cloak of assuredness I sometimes reluctantly don. It's easier to be seen, than to stay hidden and have to face questions later about "your okay-ness." So, I, like many of my colleagues, make sure I always show up. I make sure I am present. Available. Affable. Hiding my broken courage behind my abilities and eagerness to complete my tasks; yet, knowing that I could be easily exposed at the most mundane moments. No one can question your effort when you show up. Absence begets curiosity, and that breeds doubt into opinionated coworkers and superiors about "how much you actually care." Your sense of dedication is oddly on the line. Thus, you merely being there, at the dawn of death, speaks volumes to those who are awaiting your final word.

I turned the corner, my eyes savoring their short lived escape under a blink, only to find my patient's husband and son at the end of the corridor when they opened. They've never met me before, just a voice. However, as I walked toward them, seated on a small bench outside of her room, I could sense that they knew it was me approaching them. We talked; the son now standing, his hand pressed on top of his seated father's shoulder. His eyes were fixed on the shallow space in front of him; head nodding as I spoke, with a few of his own words mumbled intermittently. I wondered what he was thinking. I traveled back to my conversation with his daughter. She outlined how, after her father retired as a high-level executive, managing index funds and large detailed corporate accounts, he shifted his focus from spreadsheets to her mother. From what I could gather, my patient was vibrant and active. She filled her domestic time with a life she coyishly enjoyed, both in the public eye of her family and within the privacy of her imagination. She told me her mother kept an agenda, which was always full and always filled with "things for herself". A week after her father's retirement dinner, though, golfing and catching up on books he never finished lost their appeal. He needed a purpose, a schedule, an outline that benefited from his laser focus and keen aptitude. Thus, managing his wife's life became his new career.

At first, she didn't mind. She liked him being in control, leading. It made him happy, so it made her smile. Having him around more was supposed to be fun, and it was at first. A ride to the beauty salon? No problem, Love. Someone to check off the grocery list items? He was more than willing. They felt young again, like new lovers; him next to her, hers next to his. The sandy shores of her imagination she buried her feet in while walking through this new phase of her life, unfortunately, dissipated when she took ill a few years later. Her healing from her an abdominal surgery (to relieve an obstruction) felt scheduled and regimented. Unmet goals and complications were met with passive insinuations of her giving up or not sticking to the plan. He obsessed over outcomes and abnormal labs; she slowly relinquished her sense of selfhood and turned inward. He kept yellow note pads filled with daily routines that were later entered into precise Excel spreadsheets. Their daughter noted that afterward, her mother was never the same. Her life was a series of doctors' appointments; more tests to explain results from previous tests that resulted in more tests. It was spinning. Her father resisted any insight from others; he felt it was love. It was him giving her the very thing that afforded them the life they enjoyed for the better part of sixty-three years: his focus.

It was difficult for me to see their story, or even understand the nuances of it all. My only dealings with her were during the few days she was in my care, intubated and unresponsive. Over-breathing the ventilator, grimacing and persistently tachycardic, her eyes were static and opened to what seemed like a spaceless eternity. It almost appeared like she was afraid to blink, as if doing so would invite her to never open her eyes again. The woman before me was a shell. Someone's wife, mother, friend, and confidant, but I could not see her story. I saw her pain, her suffering. I saw her wrinkles trying to prove their worth over a body that was fighting for its life. The photos in the room helped, sometimes. Nothing, however, replaces human senses: touches, sounds, mannerisms, and voice inflections.

Disease has a selfish penchant of stealing away more from us than merely our health; it also robs us of our wellness, of our vigor. Our sense of security is penetrated, and even the echoic vibrations in our voices are hummed to a pause. It quiets us, takes away our ability to communicate the depths of our personalities and humanistic traits. In a sense, our birth rights are stolen, as is our uniqueness. Our inherent sounds, carved over years of developing our ability to speak up for ourselves and feelings, are lost in the copious sea of ventilator alarms and ECG beeping. The pages of our story are torn away, tossed into a finite pile of forgotten chapters, so that the final one can be written.

My words were heavy, but indirectly carried a defeated tone. I wanted to kneel and be sure he could grasp what I was trying to share, but something inside of him guided his aged posture to stand. He wanted to hear me clearly, he noted, because I was talking about *his wife*. I paused. Gave him the time he needed to adjust his mask, as he fumbled the unused tissue in his hands. His son looked up at him, knowing that he and I had deeper conversations about his mother's failing health. We both tried to spare his father the details of the bad news we privately discussed about *his wife*.

He repeated those words as he asked questions. He never uttered her name, as if he was trying to be sure I understand who I was referring to in my words about life and death. We were not talking about a patient or a series of labs or testing results. This wasn't about outcomes, probabilities, and mortality scores. Whatever notions his daughter indirectly etched into my psyche about their love, or their marriage, faded as he spoke. I could sense what he was trying to convey in front of people who could not possibly understand how he was feeling at that point. This was about something more, a cherished promise that may or may not have been forgotten. This was about an overlooked apology that should have shared space with grocery items and medical itineraries, but mistakenly never made the list. This was not about him, or their kids, or her medical ailments and failing health. This was about sixty-three years of his world, his love, and his life.

His tears, matching the decrescendo of my pauses between saddened news about her current state, began to slow as his blinks settled into a nervous tremor. Yet as he stood there, he made sure I overstood that he fully comprehended what I was nudgingly inferring about a woman he has loved for longer than anyone currently on the ICU staff had been alive. He shook my hand. I asked if he wanted to see some of her imaging in order to visualize the extent of her lung injury, and pneumonia. He graciously declined. What he said to me next will stay with me forever:

"Dr. Moss, you've been kind. I thank you for..." he cleared his throat "... taking care of My Wife. It is in God's hands now. You've been a great doctor. You've called me every day and I can sense that you care about her... a lot.... I can tell that you did your best. I know you haven't failed her, and I'm so glad that she had you for a doctor because you were a part of God's plan for her life. So, thank you. I know you have policies but... with all due respect, I would like to walk into this room and see... *My Wife.*"

63 years.

7

small steps.

After the Green house, we lived in a small one-level apartment, which was about a five-minute walk from my school. I recently moved in, but my mom and siblings moved there a few months before my arrival. She finally left Ulysses after getting tired of the drunken afternoons and predictable weekend fights, which were beginning to trickle over into weekday scuffles as well. I, too, was tired of it all. I was tired of calling my grandmother, Ella, each time my mother was beaten and tired of my mom getting mad at me because I called. She got so upset with me one time, she sent me to go stay with my grandmother, who lived right outside of the city limits. That lasted for a few months. I guess Joyce just needed to cool off, or leave Ulysses.

It was 1990, and I was just starting the fifth grade at North Lauderdale Elementary. I was an eager ten-year-old, who was also just starting to become happy about life. For the first time, we actually had things. Nice things. A Nintendo. Relevant memories. Street football. Christmas toys that still worked. Warm school breakfasts. Even a decent group of friends. My quick wit landed me in in gifted classes, and my primary fifth-grade teacher, Mr. Tomack, was the first person to instill the idea in me that being smart was "okay." I won spelling bees and math-a-thons in his class. Sat up front and raised my hand more than anyone else. My report cards have always said "Honor Roll," but for some reason in his class it meant more. He liked *smart Jimmy*. The Jimmy who called his grandmother when things were not right at home. The Jimmy who didn't like moving around a lot, or men coming and going in his life. More importantly, I liked that Mr. Tomack and my classmates liked me, and didn't make fun of me for being myself.

But teachers aren't parents; they are teachers. They are responsible for twenty to twenty-five kids for the early portion of the day, then it's back to your own reality. I don't know what that reality was for other kids, but for me it was finally starting to get better. My mom was dating a guy name Matt, and he was nice enough. He did his weekend beer drinking thing, but never overdid it. He was a small-statured man, with a long smile and a penchant for even longer cars. His demeanor was calm and urbane; he never raised his voice unless he was laughing or telling his side of a joke. Unlike my mother's other boyfriends and exes, he spoke to me and my siblings, took interest, and made us a part of his reality. He called Jerald and I his sons—in public and in private. We never had a "real dad," so we didn't know if he was okay with us calling him that. He erased any avertible awkwardness, though, by asking us to simply refer to him as "Matt." Also, for the first time in our lives, we received an allowance. It was Matt's idea: $10 a piece at the end of the week—if we did our chores and didn't get into trouble. On the weekends, Matt and my mom took us to flea markets and dollar stores; we flashed our money like young patrons who owned the joints. Poor kids pretending to not be poor; those moments became normal and made us feel the same. We liked Matt, a lot. Joyce did too, but Poochie not as much.

That winter, they got into a fight. About what? Who knows? It probably was Joyce being Poochie. She probably got into a fight with him because he loved her, and he probably didn't fight back because he did. So, he left. When he was gone, it felt like he took a part of me with him that I never knew existed until it was no longer there. A peace, a sense of comfort knowing that my reality was normal for a period of time. I felt what it felt like to be a kid, to not worry. I felt comfortable around him, and safe. I was embarrassed to tell my friends that the man I had hoped would become my future dad was ran off by my present mother. Not because he was bad, but because he was *too good*. Maybe *too good* to be true, and maybe that made my mother nervous. Maybe she was so used to not being loved the right way that when it finally occurred it felt wrong.

Besides, good things were not a regular part of our reality for a long time. It was always "something": a lost job, a late bill, an eviction notice, a stint living with Ella- something. Poverty was slowly gnawing away at my self-confidence. In its wake, it left a child too afraid to have too much hope in anything because "something" always took it away. Then there was Matt, this good thing. This positive "something" that replaced my wish for "anything" I could finally find solace in. This nice guy who was sober more than he was wasted, who laughed more than he yelled, and who worked more than he talked about looking for a job. When he left, the calmness he indirectly brought to my life left as well, and so did my sense of wellness. I didn't cry when he was no longer there, but I got sick.

Later in life, my mom told me that she was told I had meningitis, that I caught a "bad flu" that went to my spine. All I remember was one day playing street football with my friends that winter, the next day having a fever, and then the following day not being able to walk. I was taken to a local children's hospital, but my memory only offers me a shadow of these events. It felt like a blur. One moment I was on the couch, crying and not responding to OTC meds and aloe water, which my grandmother was convinced could evict cancer if called to do so. The next moment I was lying on a stretcher in an ER bay. I remember the pain. The nurses holding my legs and arms while the ER doctor inserted the needle into my back. The IVs in my arm that made it hard to get into a comfortable position in bed. I remember the nurses buying me little snacks and a toy car from the gift shop. One night, still unable to move my legs, this older black nurse came into my room and whispered that "we" were going to walk again. Her words were firm, yet soft. Her resemblance to a church usher, silenced my inability to disconnect her image from my youthful ideas of how a nurse should look. Tearfully, I told her, "I can't."

"You can't what?"

"I can't walk. It hurts."

"Well, if it hurts, you can feel. If you can feel, then you can move. C'mon."

Before I could offer up another complaint, she had me out of the bed and onto my feet. The cold ground soaked through my socks and sent a shock wave up my legs. Grasping her arm, with my fingers burying into the firmness of her tensed muscles, I was hoping my toes could replicate a similar feat, but the rigidness of the hospital floor had other plans. My knees repeatedly buckled, shaking with the uncertainty of what I was in that moment: a child. I felt weak and scared. Leaning on her, I asked to sit down, and she snapped, "Hey... hey, look at me." With tears in my eyes, I looked up into hers. They were deep and determined, with heavy wrinkles under her eyelids that never moved when she blinked. She started talking again, encouraging me, but I couldn't stop staring into her eyes. It felt like she was looking into my fear and asking it to leave. Her eyes were like prayers. They felt happy like my grandmother's did on Sunday mornings, on those rare occasions my mother arrived with us a few minutes early for devotional service. With her hand behind my back, and her words grabbing my ears, she repeatedly said, "There you go, just walk."

After about ten steps, I was moving again; I was walking slowly, but freely. On my own, no hand ushering me and no pain holding me back. She walked with me back and forth across the room a few more times and then let me sit down for a minute or two. Then back again. This carried on for about ten to fifteen minutes. The next thing I remember was waking up, and Ella and Joyce were in the room. I told them about the nurse that helped me walk last night, and they smiled and asked my day nurse about what occurred. Perplexed, she was unsure what I was referring to. She explained that there was no "older black, female nurse" on the floor last night; in fact, she told us that my evening nurse was a male.

"No, it was a lady. She helped me walk!" I happily proclaimed, eyes darting around, waiting for an adult's apologetic approval of my recollections of last night's events.

Eager to show them, I got out of bed and steadily started to walk across the room. My smile and shaky steps did little to change the nurse's story that my nurse was indeed a white male. My mother and grandmother brushed it off as well. They were happy I was improving, but unbothered by my dreamlike explanation of my clinical improvement. A few days later, I was discharged, without seeing my mystery nurse again to validate my claims. On the drive home, my grandmother told me it was "an angel"; I was adamant that it was old black woman. I saw pictures of angels before, I noted. I never saw one that looked like an elderly black female, in a nurse's uniform, with dark black eyes that had deep wrinkles around them.

I told my story to my siblings, but Jessica was more interested in the toy car I had, and Jerald was ready for me to open my goody bag the nurses gave me—filled with candy and extra toiletries. He took the lollipops and left the toothbrushes. I wasn't cleared for school, so I had to stay home alone while my mother went to work. One day, I heard the doorbell, and I followed my typical routine. I knew that ten-year-old kids were not supposed to stay home by themselves. Instead of answering the door, I peeked through a window a few feet down from the front entrance to make sure it wasn't the police. To my surprise, it was Mr. Tomack, with a large brown bag in his hands. He was out of class as well, one of his relatives recently died. When I cracked open the door, he greeted me with a large smile and asked if my mother was home.

"Yeah, she's asleep," I hurriedly lied.

He noted that he didn't want to wake anyone, but he asked the substitute teacher to have the class make me some get well cards and he wanted to deliver them to me personally. He handed me the package and wished me well. Closing and locking the front door, I excitedly opened it and started to cry. All of my classmates made huge cards with tootsie rolls attached to them in the forms of various art projects. Some made cars and houses, as well as basketball courts and playgrounds. Sitting on the floor, in my pajamas, I read every one. I was happy and proud that my friends really cared about me. I was alone, in an apartment, in the middle of the projects, but in my hands was proof that I mattered to people other than my family.

In that moment, something changed in me. I couldn't make sense of it, but it felt the same way I felt when Matt would call me "son", whenever he asked me a question or wanted to gather my attention. I felt the same way when my grandmother would hug me, or when I thought about my "nurse angel" who taught me how to walk again—then mysteriously disappeared. I didn't know what to call this feeling, this calmness and enlarging sense of comfort that grew deeper with every breath. As I sat there, tears falling from my face into a lap too small to catch every drop, I forced myself to embrace whatever it was I felt flowing throw my veins and brazenly rearranging my thoughts. I wasn't sure how to describe it, but it felt like what so many have said love feels like—so I called it that: Love.

Life has an inelegantly cruel way of showing you things will work themselves out, most of the time, via trials and tribulations. You live and you learn, and somehow during the process, if you're openminded and available when hope arrives, you learn how to live. I am not sure when most people experience (what they believe to be) "love" for the first time, but my initial understanding of it, at the age of ten, was pure and captured amid chaos. I remember being told that light and dark cannot occupy the same space at the same time, as a way to describe how love and hate cannot coexist in the same situation. However, at a young age, I found myself discovering love within a life I was slowly becoming to hate. I didn't like how things were, but I was finally starting to take on a perspective that gave me a sense of optimism, a glimmer of promise. People liked me and I was loved. Those two things began to chip away at the dark stains of my youthful existence. I started to realize, although I was powerless to change the darkness in my world, all I had to do to access the beauty of its light was to look within myself and create another.

interlude

little black boy

little black boy
sit down.
fold your hands into your lap
and put your lap into order
now cry me a little song.
sing me a little note about me
caring about what you care about,
then dream me a little dream.
and when your tears turn into
oases and exposed river
stand up
and pour me a little cup
fill it with every broken promise and
the unfulfilled moments of
belated birthdays and first days
of the school year when your
clothes were unkempt...then
tell me a little secret

about how—you wish your father

bothered enough to be a father or

fathered another version of you,

so that you could have a friend

and then

write me a little poem.

make me a little rhyme about

the places you lived and the schools

you've attended

the teachers you've impressed

and the classmates

you've offended...by simply

being a little black boy

who could read and speak well...

and vividly express himself,

find clean shirts amongst the dirty ones

and dress himself

long enough

to cover up his little pain

and then bring me a little more...

of whatever it is that you have...

bundled up in your little hand,

stashed away from piercing eyes,

tucked inside of your little lap

that you peek at every moment

you are given a little slack

a little chance and little hope

a little grade for your little work

just...put it in my hand...and

trust me, little black boy

i promise to give it back--in order.

ella & jimmy.

The best parts of a play usually occur off stage, behind the curtains. In between sets, there are costume adjustments and mini rehearsals. The air is thickened with unseen trivial disputes about last minute changes, which very well may enhance the audience's entire experience. This is all as much a part of the show as the characters taking a front stage bow for countless backstage efforts. The fact that it typically goes unappreciated isn't as important as the fact that it seamlessly occurs. Those who know, *know*. There is little doubt to the core team as to who the real champions are. The lighting team, the makeup artists, directors, and sound crew. The person positioning the small trays of food in the hall next to the cleaner bathrooms. The fetchers of thread and needles. The scene staff behind the scenic view. The theatrics my mother often presented to the world were readily applauded and adored. She was indeed the life of all the parties, weekly providing a reiterated update of her magma opus. But if you looked closer, if you peeked behind the curtain, if you pulled back the veil of her performance, you would see that the entire workforce literally carrying her show and keeping it from dramatically coming to end, was all being managed by one person, her mother, Ella Jackson.

She wasn't a saint, but she was a God-fearing woman. Everything about her exuded goodness; even her affinity for cursing while upset was often easily ignored. Slow to anger, quick to hug and hang compliments like summer sheets on clotheslines, Ella was the easiness within my life, the calm. There were distinct, remarkable instances, life and death events, that were halted by her merely entering the room. She was my "good thing." My constant. Jerald and Jessica had Joyce; I had Ella. Being the first grandchild, it always felt like I had "dibs," a closer bond or understanding with her. For all my mother's (obscure) disconcerting character miscues and my father's knack for absenteeism, Ella balanced it all with interjected periods of stability and togetherness. She preached the basics: family, respect, diligence, and hard work. No one listened though. When she voiced her opinions, her furrowed eyebrows scared my siblings off, and her stern faithfulness annoyed my mother's disloyal boyfriends. No one in my immediate family too much cared for her ongoing positivity either. She never accepted poverty as an excuse for not living with a rich spirit, nor did she passively nod her head whenever disagreements were in her company. She didn't always live with us back in Florida; however, she was always *there*- a pillar, a permanent fixture whenever the "going got tough" and we had nowhere else to go.

She was from a huge family (second oldest daughter of seventeen children), with an even larger name (Mack). However, Ella's admiration of Florida's sunny skies and coastline waters far outweighed the unwelcomed heat engulfing South Jersey's cornfields. So, when she was old enough to leave as a teenager, she left. I'm not exactly sure when she moved there, but I know why she stayed: Jessie Jackson. She and Jessie married for all the good and bad reasons people excused themselves for back in those days, and from what she told me, it worked. He loved her, and she loved how he loved her. She took up small jobs here and there, but once my grandfather started making "good money" driving trucks, she found herself both with child and homemaking duties. They wanted more kids, but life is amusing about giving us what we need whenever we want something else. From what her sisters would later tell me, Ella was the best of the flock, but never had a flock of her own. All of her siblings, except Willie Mae who passed away as a child, had more than one offspring. Some had eleven, some had five, some had two, Ella had one. One husband. One child. No flock.

One day, she heard a knock at the door. Maybe two. She thought it was a dream, but it suddenly became as real as the heaviness in the officer's eyes greeting her at the front door of a new reality. While trying to avoid an accident,

Jessie slammed on the brakes, and his semi-truck jackknifed and, well, there was an accident. Stepping backward, she uttered a word that Jessie never told her before. He spoiled her, gave her whatever she wanted. Car. Home. Nice things. A family. A dream. No flock, but a child and a promise. She never loved a man hard before; he was her first love and first avenue to what love could become. He was the answer to the "*Why do you stay way down there in Florida?*" question she was often asked by her family members 'Up North'. He spoke fondly of her, showered her with the kindest praises, but never uttered "that" word before, so when she said it, it came out reluctantly as if it was fighting for space in her mouth for air:

"No... no, no, no, no, no.... No! No, he's not! Stop it! Stop!"

"Ma'am, I am sorry," were the last words she remembered the officer saying.

Everything went numb. Her chest. Her fingers. The room. The officers' words and hand gestures. The chair with the loose armrest Jessie promised her he'd eventually fix that she found herself sitting in. The quietness down the hall where my seven-year-old mother lie asleep, unaware that her new reality was being awakened from a dream. She wanted a hug, an excuse to not feel. She wanted the officers to tell her they were at the wrong house so that she could accept their apologies and pray for whoever *really* lost their husband that evening, in an accident. That's what this was, an accident. This wasn't real; it was a bad dream. If she could get back to her bed, and just rest her nerves a bit, she could pray God gives her another dream, a new one. A new story to tell Joyce when she asks for her father the next morning or why he is late coming home. He's coming home. She made up in her mind that when she wakes up, she will have his favorite breakfast ready: slightly undercooked eggs, soft bacon, biscuits, and strawberry preserves. He likes coffee too; she will make sure he has some coffee. The house is already cleaned, but she will freshen it up a bit. It will be nice, just how he likes it. When he comes home it will be nice. She convinced herself that she was right, and knew she was right because she could feel her tears sliding down her face, onto her chest, that no longer felt numb.

They moved around a lot. Finding odd jobs, my grandmother did the best that she could as a single black mother in the late 60s. She turned her fifteen cents into dollars, and then traded those dollars in for a life that wasn't a fraction of the life she once knew. She dated and had her *"girl, get back out there and live yo life"* fun times, but it was never the same. Guys were nice, handsomely paid and could kiss well, but they were not Jessie. She and Joyce never spoke of the accident much; she wanted to move my mother forward without pushing her into dark places. Jessie spoiled Joyce, like all dads did with their girls, but it was a bit much—at least she thought. Kids got toys; Joyce got more toys. Little Johnny across the street got a bike; Jessie bought Joyce a riding lawn mower. Whatever she wanted, she got. Whenever Ella disapproved, she still got it. And when Jessie died, Joyce still wanted things, and when Ella couldn't afford them, well, Joyce still figured out a way to get them.

The continuous moving became a thing, steadily switching schools and changing friends. Joyce became accustomed to not staying at a place long. It became an excuse to rebel and act out. Her grades were fine, but Ella worried that not having her dad, or any siblings, was causing Joyce to inwardly create an identity she hid from the world, more importantly, from her. Ella kept her in church, but Joyce began to entertain what all church girls ignored choir rehearsals for: boys. Tough boys and bad boys. Hoodlums and boys that skipped school for extracurriculars that never showed up on report cards and such. Ella found out about one of these boys Joyce was fond of. She didn't care much for him. She would always say his smile was full of lies. The first time Joyce introduced him to her, she felt something deeply wrong in her spirit. A bad thing. An awkward vibe. A familiar feeling. A numbness in her chest. Staring at him next to my mother, on her front porch, Ella stood emotionless as he smiled. He extended his hand in her direction, boldly introducing himself with pride.

"How you doin', Ms Ella? My name is Jimmy Moss."

Big Jimmy gave me his name, Poochie proclaimed, because he always wanted a boy, which felt like a lie. She also told me Big Jimmy never wanted kids and encouraged her to get an abortion when I was conceived. Her tears didn't change his stance either, but her giving him back the money he gave her to get one was some illusion of trust between them, which never made much sense to me. He was, for lack of a better phrase, a bad boy who never became a good man. More deceiving than dangerous, more conniving than confrontational. The stories I would hear of his wrongful doings rivaled Hollywood movie scripts, which were inadvertently shipped to Hollywood, Florida, where we lived for short stint with someone else's wife. He was a smooth talker, with a smile that welcomed more hopefulness than trust. My mom would say he could "talk a fox down from a tree," followed by her own smile shadowing the hope he stole from her years after my birth.

In all earnestness, most of my memories of him are stories that seem more like fables now. Nothing was straight forward; there was always a flare or a heightened plot. The tales were never simple, like, "Big Jimmy robbed a gas station," but rather, "Big Jimmy once got a job at a gas station, moved up the ranks, became manager, and then emptied the store's safe on his first managerial shift." He was once a deacon at a small church, prancing his "Christian" family around during devotion and late-night revivals. His spiritual commitment was disconnected from his proposed plot, but the devil is always in the details. Deacon Moss rapidly became Junior Pastor Moss, hailing from the *I'm About to Rip These People Off* Seminary College. Once he gained access to the treasury, we abruptly switched churches, left town and, suddenly, he was no longer a man of God. I'm certain Joyce (and Poochie) prayed for a better life, a better path, but now with three kids from a man who walked down the valley of the shadow of death with a deck of cards, it became obvious that praying was useless. Big Jimmy never stared at the sky to gain a better grasp of "any God". The only time he looked upwards was to find trees to provide him shade from whatever light of suspicion he was trying to avoid. And if those trees had foxes, well, they were eventually convinced to come down.

As the stories of his escapades grew, the ugly truth of his reality started to add up as well. The last time I saw him I was about seven years old, and at that point I was already used to him not being around much. I remember him kidnapping Jerald and Jessica once, kind of. He picked them up from school without approval and without notifying my mom (i.e., the kidnapping), but just dropped them off at his old friend's house (i.e., the kind of). The façade of fatherhood played well into his fox-calling theatrics; but foxes, like kids, are wild and unpredictable. Imagining Big Jimmy with a backseat holding two black kid foxes was as comical as it was concerning. Kid foxes need food and sleep. Kid foxes ask questions: "Where are we going?" "What are we gonna eat?" "Where's Lil Jimmy, and Mom?" Kid foxes like Jerald and Jessica weren't quiet or apologetic about being loud. They were kids, his kids, but now also his problem. However, Big Jimmy was more of a bullshitter than a liar. Liars are deceptive; their intent is purely to gain something from you that is of vital importance to them. Money. Material items. The possession of a *thing* is their primary and ultimate goal. Contrastingly, bullshitters don't really care about *things*. Their aim is to get you to believe the bullshit. Conning you of out of twenty bucks or two biological kids is never about the money or having the kids, it's about seeing if they could actually do it. Big Jimmy did it, and that was good enough for him.

After an evening of front porch crying and phone calls, Jerald and Jessica were safely back home. No physical harm came to them. They were across town, playing outside when we arrived to pick them up. Joyce's excitement and high-pitched screams were punctuated by the fading police lights in the background. No arrests were made. Big Jimmy was nowhere to be found. His friend merely stated that he dropped the kids off "for a bit," but when a bit became nightfall, he called the local police station to make sure nothing happened to him. When he mentioned he had two kids his friend left in his possession, they matched the description my mother reported hours before. I never saw or really heard from him after that. Ulysses and Big Jimmy got into a huge fight, a turf war of sorts. I doubt they fought for my mother's hand in love or marriage. Knowing what I know now about machismo and flawed male egoism, their fight was most likely about broken black male pride and late-night drinking bragging rights. Neither of them cared about the spoils, a single black mother and her tree foxes, but rather the stories of spray-painted chivalry across our neighborhood's dilapidated walls, echoing a sense of pride that would follow them over time.

"Man, I whooped his ass."

A part of me knew that each of them uttered this phrase, and they were both right. Ulysses notably won the physical altercation, the fight, leaving a large scar across Big Jimmy's chest, which my mother would speak fondly of during late night spades tournaments she hosted after her food stamps came in. Yet, Big Jimmy won the war—he was no longer fiscally, emotionally, or parentally responsible for the three kids he sired. By losing a fist fight, he excused himself, in classic narcissistic flare, of having to deal with "Joyce and her kids." We were Ulysses' problem now. Big Jimmy talked us down from the tree and we landed in Ulysses' front yard. In his drunken states, he was probably unaware of the con, his barbaric fulfillments blinding him entirely. But when sobriety arrived, and we were looking up at him, all the while not looking like him, in need of food, shelter, and, ironically, a dad, he probably whispered to himself:

"This is some bullshit."

just breathe.

"Doc, I can't breathe."

Inhale. Exhale. So intuitive. So easy, so reflexive. Just take a breath in, then out. There is a pace to it that reflects so much about our well-being. Metabolic disarray. Impending emotional doom. Climactic disease states. How we breathe tells more than a story about how we are doing. It carries a wave of energy that either injects subjective calm into our surroundings or waves a white flag for help. We take being able to simply breathe for granted until we are reminded when we cannot. If there is any sign needed that our control of "ourselves" is finite, at best, it is buried in the entangled neuronal interconnections of the reticular activating system (RAS). This primal area of our midbrain is not well defined anatomically. It sits at the core of our arousal and conscious states, balancing sleep-wake cycles, and attentiveness, with primitive reflexes like swallowing and automatic breathing. Pathological lesions from strokes, or infections, to this part of the brain results in poorly defined comalike states, or even death. And when its well-being is threatened (e.g., during low oxygen states), the body's response is to go into full panic mode, grasping for survival's fingerlike extensions of hope, even at the expense of losing grip on reality.

We measure a person's oxygen state via two methods. The first, an arterial blood gas, samples a portion of blood from arteries to show the partial pressure oxygen is exerting on your blood vessels. The second, a pulse oximeter, is an indirect measuring tool that uses photodetectors to estimate the percentage of red blood cells that are saturated with oxygen. Obtaining arterial oxygen measurements are cumbersome (and painful, unless a patient has an arterial catheter to sample blood from), so we generally use pulse oximeters (consisting of a noninvasive probe we place on their fingers) to quickly assess a patient's oxygen status. Anything above 90% is acceptable; anything less than that (hypoxia) is borderline life threatening. And when patients feel threatened, their RAS goes into overdrive. Sometimes it causes them to rip their oxygen delivery device off, as well as their pulse oximeter. No oxygen and no means to measure a patient's oxygen levels is one of the most dangerous situations in medicine, and whenever this occurs my pager typically starts to go off.

I was consulted about this patient two days prior. Today, I find myself in his room, physically helping to restrain him, while trying to reason with him in his hypoxically confused state.

"Sir, you have to keep your oxygen on. Your lungs are filled with fluid and infection.... If you keep taking your oxygen off you're not going to do well.... Sir, no.... Sir, stop taking—" trying to hold his hands away from his face.

His nurses have been dancing this dance for a number of days. In and out of limited PPE, exhausting their patience for a patient who has been physically exhausting to care for. Begging. Pleading. Asking nicely. Asking firmly. Asking his family members for vocal guidance via Facetime. Asking me for more meds to help them help him. Ativan. Haldol. Zyprexa. Precedex. Prayer. Anything. I know it's not working. None of it is. The high-dose steroids we are administering for his acute respiratory distress syndrome (ARDS) are causing psychosis. The other drugs, having fallen off his med lists, offer a glimpse into failed attempts to induce some sense of medicinal tranquility. The low oxygen in his blood is barely bathing his already poorly vascularized brain (RAS), compromising the plaque ladened coronaries in his heart, and starving his diabetic engraved kidneys. It's a perfect storm brewing and I know what is about to happen. It's like the writing is on the wall, but I'm trying to avoid looking at the wall, even while my nursing teammates are impatiently staring at me through

CaviCide-streaked face shields, like "Really? I know he sees this gigantic wall... with words on it! Moss... HELP!"

He needs a breathing tube. A ventilator. Liters of propofol and fentanyl, most likely full-body paralysis, probably continuous dialysis, for days—if not weeks. Then he will need one-on-one nursing care, but we don't have any nurses. The one nurse who can run the CRRT (continuous dialysis) machine is in another room with her patient, who unsurprisingly danced this same dance three days ago. Now what?

I call the family, but it's an effort in futility. Their tears, their misguided ideals founded upon TV medical dramas, and their poor understanding of how bad things are truly going, collectively makes the call not worth it—but I still call. I obtain permission to do things, life saving measures, then I proceed with my efforts. This patient is dying, and his fate was sealed long before I walked into his room two days ago asking him to breathe and keep his oxygen on. My cynicism abating, I find myself sitting at the workstation phone, selfishly enjoying the quietness of the inanimate objects: landline phone, computer keyboard, mouse, etc. None of them seek my attention. However, all of them offer a momentary distraction via reflecting the very thing that is escaping me before I walk into my patient's room: stillness. When life is battling death, it is loud. Palpable. To intervene is to welcome the war and embrace the audible clamoring, pretending to not be altered or moved disconcertingly. To showcase stillness and resolve, while blocking out the sounds and remembering to breathe.

Inhale. Exhale. Sigh.

I can see the roaring madness through his ICU room's glass door. It is covered with the names of drugs that were jotted down earlier in black dry-erase markers for other nurses to grab because his nurse couldn't leave his room. I am not sure who was taking care of her other COVID-19 patients while she was in his room, but someone must have because no one has hit the code blue alarm yet. Everyone is rustling around, grabbing equipment, adjusting, and applying monitors. The respiratory therapist secures my typical setup. My other nursing teammate yells out through the cracked door, "Moss, what drugs you want?"

"The usual. Hunnid of Roc. Twenty of Etomidate. Five of Versed. Get some Levo; an epi push and a 10cc flush. Grab the code cart too."

"Can someone grab me...", she yells out through the small opening, her voice fading amongst the background noise of alarms and other voices trying to orchestrate the overwhelming sense of chaos that is ensuing. My calmed demeanor is about to be disrupted with sounds of hurried expectations. I quickly erase my frustrations with him for *not listening to me earlier*, not taking my advice that he ironically came to the hospital to receive. We are now about to dance a different dance—and a more dangerous one. I'll lead, giving him a cocktail of anesthetic poisons, hoping his failing organs play fairly and not step on my toes.

Standing behind his bed, three team members are trying to hold him still while. I try to get his oxygen levels from 70% to a respectable 80% before I attempt to take over his breathing for him. The plan: quickly exchange his slipping control of his life from his hands to mine, without any temporary exits toward death. His kicking and resisting cause his IV to come out (of course). I yell, "Grab 300 of ketamine!" so we can give it intramuscularly, just to calm him down enough to perform our tasks. Before the drug arrives, he begins to crash. His vigorous twisting is now a series of small random jerking movements. His heart rate is decreasing; his oxygen saturation is now 63%. I confirm he still has a weak pulse and quickly force the breathing tube through a puddle of thick, infectious oral secretions into his lungs. Subconsciously, I pray the seal on my mask doesn't have a small crease big enough to accommodate the toxic air he's been coughing on us for days. Cuff up. Color change. Bilateral breath sounds. Before connecting him to the ventilator, we aggressively administer high pressure breaths via a handheld Ambu-Bag device. His oxygen saturations are now in the 70s but climbing. His blood pressure is soft. Someone is able to slip in a 20g IV into his arm and we start vasopressors to improve his cardiac function. Over the next few hours, we slowly resuscitate him. With crossed fingers, we all silently hope the other patients haven't deteriorated while he was actively trying to die.

There is no applause afterward. No sighs of relief. No hugs or sense of "completeness." We all did something quite miraculous (saved someone's life), but it doesn't feel like it. It feels unauthentic and forced. It feels like we are making the abnormal appear normal, like we are postponing what's to come in exchange for an erased glimpse of what has already arrived. A pocketed sense of relief is our reward. Saving a life, oddly, means less guilt and, awkwardly, less paperwork. I have often found myself standing in patients' rooms moments after they pass away, retracing my steps and trying to make sure I didn't miss anything. However, reality eventually sorts out my unresolved emotions. Death is inevitable, but whenever it arrives to stake its rightful claim, it always feels surprising, as if we forget that no one lives forever. It's a balance we readily ignore. We become blinded by small victories that pale in comparison to the ultimate battle, which will soon have its final say—whether we are listening or not. Yet in the immediate aftermath, we are deaf to that whisper. This victory feels loud.

It's 3 a.m., but I still call his wife because I know she isn't asleep. She can't sleep; she's still numb from my call two hours ago. She and I both were ignoring the writing on the wall—but I still call. I explain how "machines are now keeping him alive." We talk about code status and how if his heart stops, he is unlikely to survive chest compressions. She says she understands, but doesn't, and encourages me to do everything, not fully grasping that we are already doing everything. It's hard to outline this path to patients' family members, partially from their lack of understanding of what futility truly means, but mostly because hope is invisible and difficult explain. Early in my career, it frustrated me that families would allow such extreme measures, when the "data" states that most of these measures aren't successful at all. Over time, however, I came to learn that it is not my place to impart my feelings into that equation. My role, rather, is to lend my objective expertise. I am paid to provide care, not dictate the value of that care. If someone wants to live forever, as insane as that sounds, they have the right to at least try. And although the tools and methods I am afforded to carry out such a task have failed 100% of the time, since everyone eventually dies, that math is not my math to understand. I am not employed to give false senses of hope, nor take hope away. I have been hired to delay the acceptance of what is to come and, sometimes, try to explain it all via phone calls.

I pause; slowly take in a few breaths. The crescendo-decrescendo rhythmic vibration of air rapidly enters my nose and then escapes from my pursed lips. Under the hint of a whistle, it reminds me of how intuitive breathing is and of the subtleness of its automaticity. How, when you let it all sink in, not think about it and just breathe, it becomes both reflexive and, if you allow it, reflective. Oxygen is the cornerstone of human life; five to ten minutes without it, the damage its absence induces becomes irreversible. What's left is a fractured vessel, still valuable to its shareholders, albeit, some parts, quite unrecognizable to its caretakers. The essence of my job, as an intensivist, is to maintain a judicious balance between oxygen delivery and utilization. That ratio (4:1) is of no concern to patients and their family members. My cerebral mathematics only makes sense if my results yield positive outcomes. If that ratio falls below 2:1, and does not quickly return to baseline, then I am faced with the humanistic tasks of exchanging math probabilities for apologies ("for your loss") that hardly ever capture the depth of my sincerity.

My patient eventually stabilizes over the evening. The following few days, however, his constant attempts to shuffle between life and death faded into a slow drift toward one side of the equation. I signed his care out to one of my partners. My "week-long" clinical obligation ended, and it was someone else's turn to take a stab at trying to alter the scale in his favor. Over the following week, unfortunately, I was informed that he eventually passed away; his family transitioned to comfort measures only and terminally removed him from the ventilator. I was not there, but I still felt like I was *right there*. In that room, in the trenches, encouraging my team to ignore the sting of defeat and continue onward. The beginning of his end started with my efforts to slow his battle noise down to a hum, only to summon the awkwardly loud sounds that often accompany fighting for someone's life. No trumpets. No fanciful harps beckoning the assistance of spiritual beings or angels to interfere and "play God", just a few desperate cries. Our calls for medications and equipment became pleas. Selfishly, we begged our patient to keep fighting for a life already reduced to machine alarms, vital sign alerts, and scattered beeps from a handful of inanimate monitors.

On TV, this all looks quite simple. In thirty to forty-five minutes, they make saving a life seem not only easy but almost impossible to not achieve. For all their flare and teledramatic equipoise, there is a small glimpse in the characters' faces that is eerily appreciable. Tears of frustration and sighs of relief, albeit staged, are often followed by deeper breaths and moments of reflection. Their musical scores add an element I am not afforded in similar situations, but deep inside there is still a melodic tone that I can almost hear when death enters the room. When it arrives, your eagerness to ignore its presence, while simultaneously acknowledging its grasp on whatever waning residue of faith that remains, carries you for a bit. But you are human, your strength has a finite end. Your brilliance has both its limits and its endpoint, where all that you know will eventually succumb to all that you don't.

It is in those moments that breathing becomes more than an automatic gesture. It becomes a primitive sign, proving—even in the face of pulselessness—that my pulse is still deeply engaged in helping return my patients their own. Sometimes I do so by helping them to breathe. Sometimes it's via whispering in their ears that they still have something worth breathing for. Regardless of the outcome, I rest peacefully when my time with them has ended, either through the completion of a work week or through a phone call with their loved ones. I know when they needed help at their most vulnerable state, I gave my all and, more than likely, a lot more. Not for accolades. Not for a paycheck. Not for an aimless leap for postwar applauses and indelible appreciation of my team's efforts. What I do and what I give is not a rehashed reality script, typed right before the shift started. It's not twelve hours condensed into forty-five commercial-free minutes. This is not *Chicago Med, ER,* or *Grey's Anatomy.* This is real. And for my team and others who enter ICU arenas across the country, similar to mine, day in and day out, it has become our new normal. Instinctual. Tangible. And, to a degree, intuitive.

Like breathing.

11

yin & yang.

I t's hard to tell my story without telling my brother's story. I can't tell it accurately because his version of "his truth" is inarguably more authentic than mine. My sister and I were close, but he and I shared a bond that grays the line of togetherness. We were total opposites but magnetic; Yin and Yang, but both sections were black. Jerald was my biggest challenger and cheerleader. He bragged about my accomplishments with a boastful spark that vibrated so passionately, his audience couldn't differentiate how much of it was myth or truth. His truth. My success felt like his success; however, it would be a lie if I pretended there were not times it felt like his smiles carried a regretful sense that my achievements (wins?) reminded him of his failures (losses?). Like all siblings, we bickered, fought, stubbornly liked the same girl at times, but we never hated one another. I, the big brother, was always looking out for his best interest, even when I unknowingly made him feel smaller than just being a *little* brother. Our love was different; it felt like two prize fighters hugging after nearly trying to kill each other for ten rounds. Yet even this felt odd because, although in his eyes I was always the victor, in my eyes he was the better fighter.

Jerald was always a better fighter. I guess you can say he was a better winner, as well, because he won all his fights. Quick tempered? Maybe. Instigator? Possibly. Eager to prove that fighting was a domain he readily entered and seldomly left? Always. He had small hands, the chubby kind that church mothers called *husky*, but he swung big and hard. We had our usual brother-to-brother combats; it often felt like he knew I wouldn't seriously fight back, but he wanted me to. I wasn't sure if he wanted to win to prove some ill-guided point, or if he wanted to see if his big brother, his biggest idol, his biggest shadow, could actually lose.

When I was in the fourth grade, I temporarily moved in with my grandmother. I wanted it to be permanent, but any extended time away from mom and her men felt nice—so I settled for whatever time I was afforded. Jerald would come to visit on weekends. He never asked why I was there and why he wasn't, and I was glad because the answer was probably more complicated than he or I could possibly comprehend at the time. One weekend, I was asleep on the couch in the living room and heard yelling and screaming outside the front window. Pulling back the off-white lace curtain, I saw him on one end of the line, and five other boys his age, lined up, single file, waiting their turn to fight. Earlier that day, we learned that someone "egged" my grandmother's front door, and the line of boxing amateurs outside of the living room window was Jerald's solution to the problem. One by one they stepped up; one by one, they lost. I stared at the commotion from the inside; smiling, but also too in awe to move. As the boys scattered ahead of the dust they rudely left behind, Jerald stood there assertively. Proudly protecting an egg-yoked front door of an apartment where he didn't even have a room.

That difference between the two of us, my cautious fearsomeness vs. his reckless abandon, came to define our brotherhood. For all my quick-witted, analytical abruptness at times, Jerald's physical and dominant approach was more direct, and, during our childhood, arguably more effective. He wasn't a bully, but his fists were powerful enough to ward off any extra noise not easily quieted with playground verbal exchanges. No one bothered him, and as a result, no one bothered us. We shared friends as frequently as we shared clothes; however, in the same sense, when it came to friends: he usually stuck with what fit him, and I did the same.

There was no camaraderie vacancy, though; nor any real need for outsiders to approve our existence. We both recognized each other's talents despite our flawed childhood. He was great at many things. Baseball. Football. Basketball, at times. He could rebuild broken appliances and memorize songs without needing to perfect subtle nuances, as I did. In so many ways he was "just better than me"; however, many of the areas he outperformed me in required support (rides to games, equipment, someone in the audience, actual appliances, etc.) that we simply didn't have. The sport I excelled in, basketball, was as much a solo venture as it was a unified team. I could go outside for hours, alone, and shoot jumpers or practice new moves, lost under the prism of my own rainbow. Escapeville. I would systematically trace my mistakes while trying to "be better." Me. A ball. A court. A quiet place. I was content there, satisfied that my only competition was my last shot and the sun's thievery of light. It was a safe haven; a bridge between who I was in those moments and who I wanted to become: a star, a light, a glimmer of hope. I wanted to be, and sometimes felt like, a moon without scars; a celestial force pulling gravity away from the seashores of a teenage mind that felt "stuck" and weighed down by problems I didn't create. Whenever I had a basketball in my hand, I felt like I had a chance. I had something reminding me I could be bigger and better than the limited options life was daily ripping away from me like pages in its instruction manual. My brother didn't have that. He had me.

The weight of being the oldest child can be daunting. You are expected to be some type of quasi leader, a second or third parent, sometimes even the first, without any true insight to derive your guidance from. So, you wing it. Often you are the larger child. Your intelligence and adolescent wisdom are owed to shear hormonal explosions and having received whippings for things your younger siblings were foolishly contemplating. I was two years older than Jerald, but not always bigger. My bigness was in my timid reservations. No one really knew what I was thinking, or that I was afraid many times, so the assumption was "he's more mature." However, my brother's willingness to adapt more quickly to our unwelcome societal norms was both a gift and a curse. A gift, in that he was more of a protector than I was. I mean, no one bullied the guy who beat up the bullies. Yet, his curse was buried in the same hands and furrowed eyebrows that scared off our neighborhood predators for years. Despite his good-humored nature, Jerald was depicted as the bad guy, the bad child, the anti-Jimmy, the black Yang.

After our fight with Ulysses (I say "our," because Jerald was fighting for us as much as he was fighting for our mother), my mom stayed a little longer. Their fights became a regular occurrence. His drunkenness caused him to swing a punch that came earlier than those he customarily threw. When she finally had the courage to leave, the same hands she used to shield herself with from his assaults, were now weakened from neuropathy. She worked less and less, fell into depression, and her "men" became more vital to her (and our) survival. Other than Matt, they were merely empty pages between lengthy chapters. Jessica was too young to appreciate all of this, but Jerald and I weren't. As my mother strayed away from parenthood, our brotherhood solidified and established deeper roots. He fought for me with his hands, I fought for him with my words. Moss boys. Fighting the same fight but losing different battles. I saw the brokenness of our world through a lens that was quite large; the more we moved, the more I absorbed. Houses were becoming hopscotch squares, each one lasting only long enough for me to remember their colors. I never asked Jerald what he saw. I somehow felt like he trusted my vision, my explanation of what eviction notices meant, and why we never stayed at the same schools for long stretches of time.

As time went on, his fierceness started to overcome his inner brilliance. Whenever he was questioned, he fought. Fighting led to suspensions, and that led to a disdain for school. When school became an afterthought, all the after-school programs (sports, clubs, etc.) that were designed to keep kids like us out of the streets became afterthoughts as well. But we were young then, foolish enough to believe the world was smaller than it essentially was. Although our imaginations were impregnated with boyish mischief, as far as we could tell, the dangers of the street life were imaginary ideas captured on TV. We watched *Boyz n the Hood*, not knowing we were *literally* the little boys in the hood. South Florida had more sun than guns back then, so tough guys like Jerald were safely shooting more basketballs than bullets. He loved the energy, though; the playground clearing and being picked onto teams because he was the biggest guy on the field. I found myself becoming quieter as he became larger, in both size and rumored war stories. It gave him the space to be himself, regardless if he truly understood what to do within that space. I now realize that my stepping aside, to him, was me leaving him alone. And the worse place for a fiery, ill-tempered, preadolescent black boy—living on shattered streets filled with more broken glass than hope—to be positioned in back in the late 80s-early 90s was alone.

The one and a half years that stretched between our ages always felt disruptively disjointed. Yes, from a calendar perspective, we were a mere eighteen months apart, but in sibling math, I was two years older. Those two years lead to moments of consternation when, being the oldest, I had to help or instruct a "little" brother who grew to have a larger waistline than my own. How do you tell your not-so-smaller kid sibling, who often won the fights that were started between you two well before fists were thrown, to be quiet, or clean off the table? I had to be smooth in my approach, slick with my salutations and words. I had to figure out how to make cleaning up seem like it was something *we* had to do, as opposed to something *he* was supposed to do. I learned early on that it was easier to befriend your future opponent before they even became your opponent. My tone and pitch had to be reserved, welcoming at times, like, "we are in this together", "we are cleaning up *your* mess". It was a constant game of leading without being overbearing in order to keep peace between Jerald and I, and to keep Poochie from corporally intervening.

My earlier dealings with Jerald taught me a lot, about life, about living. However, it mostly outlined the importance of finding balance, even within the fragments of a birthright. As the oldest, I innately understood I had a duty to lead my siblings; yet there were so many voids our birth parents failed to fill that it almost felt like failure was inevitable. I had no idea how to fix the mismanaged project of our lives while simultaneously growing up in the projects. I liked being the oldest, but I hated not having an immediate teenage elder, or a male elder in general, giving me tips on what to do next. These feelings were hard to make sense of at nine and ten years old. I wanted to be a kid, but I had to trade it all in to be a big brother/parent. My closeness to Jerald made it easier; I mean, for all his bravado, he was still the closest thing to normal I had on a day-to-day basis. My fraternal twin, who took two sibling years to be born, was also my first best friend. However, he needed me in ways that made it hard for me to appreciate just how much I needed him. He was my first audience member in my first venture into "becoming a leader." Always clapping, always cheering; yet, also, always waiting for me to prove my spot. It felt like I had to be both brother and dad, disciplinarian and friend, peacekeeper and parent-whisperer, Jimmy and his Yin.

As we followed each other throughout childhood, me a few steps ahead as the quiet leader, Jerald a few steps behind protecting my back in the process, poverty followed us as well. All the moving became normal, so we stopped talking about it. Our last stint in Florida came in the early 1990s, on the non-beach side of Pompano Beach. Before moving there, we were evicted from a somewhat decent apartment complex across town because of housing violations. Apparently, you can't have an ex-felon boyfriend living in your two-bedroom apartment—with three kids—if the government is footing most of the bill. I'm unsure if Poochie knew this, but Joyce most certainly did. We eventually settled into a small white house a few blocks from one of my mother's close friends. I don't remember much about it other than the parties my mother threw and the hurricane that summer (1992), which left a hole in the back window in the room Jerald and I slept in, that was never correctly repaired.

I also remember sitting outside in the front yard one day; it was December. Florida had sunny days year-round, which you never fully appreciate until you eventually leave the state. Yet, the sun came prepackaged with mosquitoes and sticker pearls. We avoided them, mostly; however, that one day they were more pestering than usual, as if they knew something we didn't. My grandmother came over and was on the phone for about an hour. As she was talking to one of her sisters, her smile extended from the front door she was standing in, phone cord tight wired above the living room floor. Her conversation ended with a few more smiles and, particularly, one question. One that would shake the very fabric of every thread holding my young life together at the time.

"Ya'll wanna move to Jersey?"

interlude.

count the ways

how do i love thee?
allow me to
count the ways,
one......... two........ three
hundred and sixty-five days
i sit adjacent from my thoughts.
thoughts of you and i
sitting closer, in love....
so i can trace it when we walk
i got... places for us to talk,
if you feel like conversating.
and even though
"conversate"
is not a word...
when i'm with you,
that's all i hear: not a word,
just silence.
and possibly the sound of

me tapping on your door,
bringing you.... the
bluest of violets...
and the reddest of roses,
with cards attached that say
just how much i love you
because how i love you
is brilliant...
and without reasoning,
or excuses....it just happens.
a sudden occurrence, like...
listening to soft music,
on the calmest of evenings,
and just clapping...
no words, no..............
significant gestures,
just us both
being involved...
trying to appreciate
our true value.
us.... investing time into
each other.... until what we have
appreciates, and accrues value
and interests-
my.... interests....
are compounded,
when i put my interests in you.
and this is more than me
telling sky and moon
how much i love you....
this is me,
submerging all my affection,

and sensible senses in you.
i'm so convinced that
what we have
is lovely... that i've filled out our
census, then moved
all unguided emotions
towards directions
opposite of our divinity.
this.... idea, poetic fragment,
scattered throughout time
and a motionless infinity...
has become affiliated with my all;
so, i give you my life;
all things peaceful,
and all that's left....
all that's me, and
all that's configured
within the confines
of all my depth-
because how i love you,
is beyond numbers...
outside of time.... and far
from breath.
thus... even when this life...
escapes our paths....
i shall but love you better
...after death.

13

---

sick days.

How do you share your war stories when you never knew you were in a war? How do you diagnose PTSD when the scars are as invisible as the trauma? My mother had lots of scars. Some she openly shared, but many I doubt she even knew existed. One of her biggest scars was her sickness. She was sick when I was a child, not *sick sick* or deathly ill, but sick. Among other non-debilitating ailments, she had (as she defined it) "bad diabetes." Not longstanding diabetes or brittle "difficult to control since a child, always in the ED" diabetes, but "Hey, you need to lose some weight because you have" diabetes. A horrible disease but manageable. Yet, her ignorance of its silent, deadly crawl caused her already failing grip on life, which she called "bad neuropathy in her hands," to weaken a bit more. She told everyone her doctor said, "She couldn't lift more than five pounds," so she stopped working entirely, even at the jobs that required only four pounds of lifting. I was around ten, or eleven, when she started telling these stories. Scar stories that sounded more fantastical than promising. They all ended the same, with this idea that being unemployed was not her fault, but rather because of her "bad diabetes." Her neuropathy. Her being tired all the time. Her being sick.

Sickness has a beguiling way of blurring lines of objectivity. The disease state can be objectively real and, in its entirety, altogether encompassing. However, the labs, x-rays, and exam findings only tell part of the story. They only provide the listener aimless evidence, or proof, that the most important pieces of the tale, the subjective aspects (i.e., what someone feels and experiences), which are clearly the most afflicting, are real. When someone says, "I don't feel well," our sympathies only extend as far as the person's ability to provide some type of verification. If you have back pain, and it's due to a very true, albeit unmeasurable and invisible, muscle spasm: tough it out. If your back pain was caused by stage four breast cancer, which has metastasized to the spine: cue sad faces, truckloads of concern, and Hallmark cards. You can't measure cancer "bone" pain, but it's visible and familiar. You can read radiological reports, count the metastatic bone spots, and cut and paste photos of how horrible it is. Our senses can empathize the results; we can "feel sorry" because we would want someone to feel sorry for us, should we come to share a similar fate. My mother didn't have breast cancer, nor did she have back spasms or photographable bone pain. She had diabetes. Bad diabetes.

As much as it is a blood sugar (glucose) disease, it is also a blood vessel disease. Unchecked, elevated glucose levels in the blood stream slowly damages microvessels. Then it challenges the larger, more impressionable, ones: cardiac, renal, and even delicate brain blood vessels, which can lead to strokes and intracranial vascular hemorrhaging. The larger blood vessel damage can cause severe disabilities, requiring heart surgeries and a permanent need for dialysis. This also takes nearly decades to occur. The former (i.e, microvessel disease) can occur in a matter of years, leading to neuropathy and minor GI issues, causing hand tingling and pain, mild nausea and vomiting—but typically not work stoppage. Early in her course of dealing with diabetes, my mother suffered from several minor diabetic complications. To prevent the major, and more ominous, problems as noted above, she was advised to improve her lifestyle choices, implement a better dietary discipline, exercise, and lose weight. She was also strongly advised to adhere to a strict medication regimen with close medical follow-up. However, to the best of my knowledge, and from conversations with my grandmother after my mother's passing a few decades later, she did none of these things. But she did stop working.

Every adult in the *hood* knew that if you could convince the government that your medical illnesses were severe enough to prevent you from working, you could get a disability check every month. Poochie's ailments were minor, but the more she told her story, the more visible her scars became. She would lie on couches and moan for hours during the week; however, on the weekend, her bad diabetes and associated ailments miraculously vacated the premises. Playing spades didn't require five pounds of lifting, just a few beers, curse words, willing playing partners, and an ability to talk smoothly after you claimed your "books" each round. Her scars faded and were never mentioned during such raucous moments. The laughter emanating from our kitchen table during my mother's weekend charades was epic and emphatically loud. It was far less disturbing than the weekday stomach moans that often sat there with my siblings and me, keeping us company as we stared at cold food we didn't pretend to enjoy. She never "let us go to bed hungry," but we didn't want boring, unassuming "weekday" food. We wanted the food my mother and her friends had on Saturday evenings when her diabetes wasn't all that bad.

Little did I know my mother's dance to manipulate the "system" out of a check each month was slowly becoming the end of my childhood as I knew it. Soon, I would have to trade in my understanding of the world and its anxious excitement of my arrival. In school we were told that tomorrow was ours for the taking, that we could be anything we wanted. As I became stronger academically, it gave me hope that I could truly become somebody. And I wanted to—badly. I wanted to be a lot of things, many things, anything, but not a preteen adult. When you're a kid, diabetes sounds as deathly as halitosis. It scared me hearing her medical problems out loud, and my mother echoed them a lot.

"I have really bad diabetes."

"I have bad neuropathy and... gastroparesis."

"The doctor said I can't work."

Everyone believed her. We believed her. Why wouldn't we believe her? I certainly believed her because that is what her *doctor* said, and to an eleven-year-old kid, whatever the *doctor* said was most assuredly correct. No one wants to be sick, so who would lie about how sick they are? Why would a mother *not want* to work and provide for her kids? Joyce wasn't the best mother in the world, at times, but she certainly wasn't the worst. I based that framework on some of the horror stories I heard from other kids in my neighborhood, troubling stories of prolonged moments of abandonment and physical abuse. Some of my friends didn't have parents at all. Many of them were repeatedly shuffled around in foster systems and hoarded away in relatives' homes that didn't have enough room to house them, let alone love them. Joyce was a lot of things I wished my childhood thoughts never entertained, but she did love us. I know she loved us; she told us. No mother who loves their kids would ever conceive a plan to exaggerate her illnesses, not work on purpose, survive on government-issued assistance (at merely a fraction of what could have been earned working at even the most lowly paying jobs), and subject their kids to years of decrepit living conditions and poverty. That's insane. That's ridiculous. That's probably one of the most inconsiderate and foolish approaches to securing a solid foundation for yourself and your children's well-being. That is borderline childhood emotional and mental abuse; heartlessly cold and hopelessly sickening. Yet, that is exactly what my mother, unbeknownst to herself, unfortunately did.

She was a good person, I believe, but she was lost. No other adults around me, other than my grandmother, had enough courage, or gall, to tell her, "Joyce, this is wrong." So, they said nothing. They came over for spades tournaments and first-of-the-month parties. They went to the clubs and chased men (who were too drunk to chase women) across town with her. They sat on our couches and asked us to fetch beers and second servings of food; never questioning whether our rations were limited or not. Poochie was well loved and well liked; she had more friends than enemies, and even her enemies still smiled in her face. I was too young to understand the gravity of her decision to "not work," so in my eyes, her fun side made up for her bad side. I hated running short on "nice food," but we always had food. Even when our living situations in Florida were horrible, she never left us stranded—at least not without some type of adult supervision (usually Ella). However, her pursuit of permanent unemployment signaled a major shift in our livelihoods. With no money, we constantly were behind on bills. Moving every six to eight months, always having to ask someone for something, like a ride to the store or recipe items to complete a meal. Joyce's bad diabetes was making everything else bad as well. Financially, it left us in dire straits, but individually it robbed me of my childhood and left me in emotional debt, which took me decades to pay off.

The first payment (of many) was due on December 23, 1992, the day we arrived in New Jersey. Our arrival signaled the end of a very difficult primary phase of my youth. From front row, ringside seats of unwarranted domestic disputes, to misguided attempts to fit into a world that didn't seem to have enough space, my childhood—like my mother—was scarred. My preadolescence memories were filled with hard lessons ripped from faded instruction manuals. This is how you survive; this is how you make do. Poochie's parenting failures matched Joyce's feelings about her life: three kids, no father for them to call Dad (nor a father for her to call, either), no replacement that truly cared, and no escape from the heaviness of it all. Florida gave her, and us, its final eviction notice; rent was due, and we didn't have it. Joyce wasn't working and Poochie didn't care. Big Jimmy was in jail, again; all my mother's ex-men were probably there too. Ella was a sensible source of hope, a retreat. However, the "good money" ($400/week) she made cleaning houses under the table was good enough money for her, but it certainly was not enough for "us." Thus, suddenly, for the first time in my life, as a twelve-year-old boy, I felt the indirect pressure of directly needing to become a man.

Her and Ella's decision to move to NJ was a welcomed surprised. We always considered "our cousins Up North" as some form of royalty we could lay claim to in our imaginations. Their big houses and large population size diluted any obvious problems they may have had. Each of my grandmother's siblings were there, except one, and everyone seemed to be doing relatively well, or at least not bad. I wasn't sure if they had a lot of money (*I bet they sure have more than we did*, I remember thinking), but they clearly had each other. Our few visits during summertime family reunions offered a small glimpse of their happiness. We would house hop to our cousins' homes, run in their large yards behind multistoried, what appeared to be, Victorian-style castles, and gleefully hide in their endless basements (something foreign to us in Florida). They were short-lived and exhaustingly fun, but those moments erased the residual pain of poverty for an entire week. My extended family was filled with all hugs and warm gospel-like voices, welcoming and charitable. They were church folks with benevolent smiles, begging us to comeback before our rental minivans left their driveways; promising that what we felt was not only genuine, but also ours. Our lease was up in Florida, and NJ, we believed, was accepting applications.

The vastness of the open fields, moving at a pace my eyes could barely manage to trace, became numbing. There were fields and more fields, some with cows and other farm animals—and some with just more fields. I wondered if the animals could feel the same bustling power, vibrating under their hooves, which I absorbed for the last twelve hours from my seat on the train. I didn't know which states we were traversing at the time, but I knew we were getting close to our new place to call home. I thought about what and who we were leaving, some memorable friends and a couple cool moments. Florida wasn't all bad, but it didn't have enough good to truly be missed.

With my face pressed against the glass, I tried to count how many cows I could see between each passing fence post, but I lost count every time we hit a rough patch of train tracks. Every bump caused me to bounce up a bit, sliding my face away from its resting spot by a few inches. I forced myself to press harder against the glass, hoping that my repositioning would give physics a run for its money. Glancing over at my grandmother, asleep from having to deal with the three of us, I smiled, happy that the plan was for us to take the train to NJ with her (and not my mom). Poochie, Terry (her boyfriend at the time), and Frankie, her best friend from since forever, drove our items up in a U-Haul. We didn't have much, and for some reason we felt we didn't need much. We were going to NJ, Up North, with my grandmother's people. If we needed anything, well, then they would probably help us out.

Jessica and Jerald, sitting across from my grandmother and me, were in a deeper sleep than she was, bodies bouncing rhythmically with the bumps my eyes tried earlier to avoid. After a series of what felt like endless red-light-green-light games, the train's final red light abruptly took me by surprise. Looking outside of my window, eyes no longer losing their race, the outside images (of people now) slowed accordingly to a stop. My first settled sight, though, wasn't a memorable image of something identifiably reminiscent of our first moment in our new home state. Instead, it was a sign that read: Welcome to Delaware.

Stepping off the train as new northern residents was eye-opening. The air was cold in a manner that I never experienced before. Wearing real coats for the first time, my siblings and I moved quickly inside, confusingly following our grandmother's hurried pace to secure our luggage. We went from warm train, to shivering cold, to back inside the warm train station waiting area so fast, that I couldn't savor the first time watching my breath humidify the air immediately in front of me. This cold was different, and taught me, unrelentingly, that whatever I thought was cold back in Florida was merely just "kind of cool outside." Every time the waiting area door swung open, we balled up and laughed as the cold breeze whistled around our playfully frozen poses, with our giggles and semi-fake shivering capturing everyone's attention.

Our December afternoons back in South Florida were a cool 70 F. The thermometer on the wall showcasing the temperature outside of the Delaware train station read 27 F. Oddly, there was no snow. I couldn't seem to piece together why it was really, really cold, but the ground was dusky and light brown, instead of piercing white from blankets of snow like I imagined. Looking over at my grandmother, I could see a slight hint of frustration on her face. She was at the payphone, rummaging through her small, little black phone book she kept in her wallet, running out of patience and, nervously, out of quarters. When she sat down next to us, searching in her purse for her gloves and a few pieces of church candy to settle down our laughter, I asked, "Who's coming to pick us up?"

Handing each of us a peppermint and a small red strawberry-shaped piece of candy she calmly said, "Somebody's coming. Don't worry, somebody's coming."

light switch.

S ome of the more difficult situations I've experienced, as a physician of color, were the encounters with *select* patients who don't expect you to be "the doctor." I've been everything in this field that I've never applied for: the janitor, the tech, the nurse, the trash taker-outer, and the help. It's an understood ugly part of the training you come to accept, never willingly but always begrudgingly. Getting accepted into medical school is a big deal for most students, but for most black students it becomes a defining ancestral moment, an echoed result from prayers sent "way before you were born." Our parents and grandparents told us stories about being on the wrong side of all the fences and all the stories. From the human stains of police brutality to the cold shadows of segregated schools (i.e., if they attended school at all), the remnants of a time lost somehow seem to find their way into all our success novels.

Stories. We all have them; some short, with magical allures weaved into their plots. Some of them are quite long, burdened with the vibration of life's ills that can neither be shaken off easily, nor explained with multisyllable words. If you ask most physicians of color, "*how has your 'color' impacted your training?*", you may get a long pause before an answer. We are cautious to not pull race cards, but the cards you are dealt are sometimes the only cards you have on hand. Our cards are colorful, shuffled slowly and cut twice. They are held close to our white coats; black *aces* next to red-and-blue blood-pumping *hearts*. Although small in number, our *clubs*, filled with *diamonds* in the rough, are always present.

Sometimes faded into the crowd, bluffingly displaying the façade that we are more ready than we appear. However, even if we are opting to not play the game, it does nothing to prevent others around us from dealing us in, regardless if the others are our patients.

My third year of medical training was in a small town in southern Georgia called Thomasville. Distinctly quaint, and eerily quiet, it shared the same similarities as most small towns in the South. However, there was a blinding line of separation among races and wealth; that is, if you were brave enough to speak up about it, or even open your eyes. Large antebellum homes towered over small sharecropping-sized houses; the rich were very rich, and the poor were very close to having a front yard view of just how poor they were. The hospital I trained at, Archbold, was near the center of the southeast of town. It was distinctively aged, but it had a charm that made if feel new and livelier than it appeared. All my precepting physicians were nice and welcoming. More notably, our racial and cultural differences never entered the conversation—and for that I was appreciative. They taught me about the abstract art of medicine, patient-centered care, and many of the required items outlined in my core curriculum. In our down times, I would pick their brains about jobs or different specialties, hopeful for insight about salaries and career stressors they wished they would have avoided. But they never obliged. It was all good things about medicine and the profession itself, which isn't necessarily a bad thing, except I was beyond the scope of mysticism about anything in life. From a young age, I learned that half of what you see is what you perceive, and all the rest is probably some fraction of a truth you will never fully understand.

The rotations only lasted a month; surgical and nonsurgical specialties, scattered amongst mandatory primary care fields: family medicine, internal medicine, pediatrics, OB, and, lastly, psychiatry. The latter was my least favorite but unarguably the most interesting. In hindsight, I wish I took more notes and paid more attention, but the intangible human diseases of the brain didn't capture my attention back then. Schizophrenia, depression, bipolar, and various affective disorders were dynamic and intriguing enough to read about, but their causative factors were not measurable. The subjective nature of "how someone acted/felt" made it hard to master the nuances of the specialty at such a ju-venile stage of my training. As a medical student, I wanted something I could memorize or recite on rounds, something unquestionable. If someone's blood pressure is low, it's low. If they are actively bleeding, they are bleeding. There was no speculation or Diagnostic Manual of Mental Disorders, Fifth Edition (i.e., DSM-V- the standard classification guideline book used for determining a patient's spectrum of mental health disorders) list of potential names for most of the diseases I saw and loved treating in the hospital. Heart failure was heart failure; sepsis was sepsis. Once you had a problem, it was usually clear, and recordable. The causes varied, but the disease itself was quantifiably something I could absorb. However, when someone came in for their psychiatric appoint-ment, I didn't know if they were having a bad day or if they were on the verge of a total breakdown. That frightened me, not for myself, but for the mere fact that I felt powerless to help them. I could not calculate their problems, so I was unable to provide an answer that would ultimately fix their broken equation—especially when the variables were all subjective.

The objective aspects of the rotation—the staff and the providers—were oddly my favorites. The two physicians I worked with, Dr. Tom and Dr. Lee, were regularly attended by Ms. Kim, their nurse practitioner teammate. They were all uniquely their own type of clinician, but their patience and calming demeanors were uniformly shared. Patients would come in with a hidden box of issues, and they would slowly piece it all together, sorting out particular feelings or thoughts into formal diagnoses that made sense. I would mistakenly find myself conflating items or overthinking aspects of a patient's history of present illness. My aim was to fit people into easy-to-understand compartments, more so for myself and the luxury of my own mental tranquility. It was primarily me opting to rationalize their issues in a manner more digestible for myself, than the other way around. After I would present my thoughts to one of the above noted providers, they would entertain my sporadic and fleeting ideas, but eventually outline a course of action that would ultimately serve in the patient's best interest, instead of my own.

Psychiatry, albeit challenging and outside of the prism of other (sub)special-ties (with their numerous testing modalities to support their findings, which could be cut and pasted into the patient's electronic medical records), did share in the one universal tenet that never escapes the tightening grip of all forms of medicine: disease is nondiscriminatory. The mutual honesty of ailments is that although they may occur more readily in one population of people (vs another), no one type of people, or race, can escape the inevitability of it all. Our bodies are designed to fail, as are our emotions and how we manage our thoughts. Depression is often shunned within some cultures, ignored, and blanketed in prayers or ritualistic endeavors. However, its stain is very much human. Along with many other psychiatric disorders (e.g., seasonal affective condition; maniac bipolar states), it has arguably played significant roles in the outcomes of pater-nalistic wars during the span of mankind. Even more, it has possibly contributed to many civil disputes and the writing of prejudiced constitutions that govern entire societies. For as mighty as we like to think we are, our mind is as fragile as the senses we use to connect it to the world around us. Sometimes that connection is broken before we ever gain a full grasp that it even exists, but that brokenness shares a similar fate that all humans must endure.

I saw all types of people during my rotation, from Hispanic migrant workers trying to understand "visions", to African American prisoners painting the sky in front of them with hand movements, which told a clearer story about their "bad thoughts" than their vocabularies allowed. I learned a lot, but it was mostly because I listened a lot. Dr. Lee, who I shadowed more than the others, was my favorite. A medium built, Asian American male, with a smile that never lasted longer than his handshake, he saw patients in an office that mirrored a busy library, which had a scattered excess of books that had no place to go. His desk was a rich mahogany, thick legged and narrow. The leather chair behind it matched the maroon accent wall behind the chair. The wall held his diplo-mas and various awards; there were a few pictures of the neighboring hospital (Archbold), although his clinic was funded mostly by the state. He was never in a hurry, but he spoke in brief spurts; every word was meaningful as if, when he released it, he positively understood it would never come back. His sense of duty and reserve was rather puzzling at first. I couldn't tell if he was over-interested in his patients' stories, or if his furrowed brow while listening was some type of faux expression of intrigue, used to rush along the visit. Yet, over time, his compassion and service were unquestionable. Whether his patients were being honest or openly lying (I could never tell) never seemed to alter his professionalism. He cared. He was present. He was neutrally objective in the face of the doubt shared by both his patients and, quite often, myself, as I sat quietly in the back of the office trying to catch every single word he tossed in my direction.

The routine was simple. Once a patient arrived in the waiting area, I was alerted to their arrival (by a secretary; there was a medical assistant but whenever a med student was present, their duties shifted to one of us), and I would call their names from the waiting room door, escorting them to a small intake area. Seated, I would perform my history (there was no physical exam) and review any new complaints, medications, or recent hospitalizations. Once I gathered said information, I would quickly organize my jumbled notes and ideas into some semblance of a plan. Next, I would discuss my findings, diagnoses, and recommendations to the provider. Sometimes my assessments were right, but frequently they were incorrect. However, the trials and errors never shook my assurance. I improved over time and found myself seeming slightly confident in my ability to look past my feelings and preconceived notions (about mental health), while presenting well thought out treatment plans that were more acceptable and clinically appropriate.

One Friday, toward the end of my rotation, I was asked to see the last patient of the day. It was 4:25 p.m., and Dr. Lee's 4:40 p.m. follow-up visit (a patient he was seeing for Dr. Tom) arrived early. I opened the waiting room door and saw an elderly white (petite) female, accompanied by a middle-aged male, both fixated on the TV show that was playing. Assuming she was the last visit for the day, I called out, "Ms. Jones?"

With the male's assistance, she feebly rose to her feet, leaning on his steadiness for balance. She glanced at me and then stared at him, whispering something into his ear. He nodded his head and proceeded to head in my direction, guiding her with a parental-like patience, each step shadowing her small shuffles he wished were a fraction of a step larger. I quickly looked down at the chart I was holding, trying to convey I didn't mind waiting for their arrival:

82 F, Hx of CAD, Diabetes, Depression and Dementia

Meds: ASA, Metformin, and Zoloft

Allergies: Namenda (causes "shakes"); Penicillin (hives)

"Ms. Jones, pleasure to meet you. I am Jimmy Moss. I am the medical student assisting Dr. Lee today." I briefly extended my hand but pulled it back when I noticed she was transfixed on maintaining her grip on her walker. The male noted that he was her son; I followed them to the intake room and closed the door.

"So how are you feeling today, ma'am?" I asked.

She remained quiet, lips urging themselves to follow her instincts. Her son looked at her and paused, gathered himself under a sigh, then turned to me and proclaimed, "With all due respect, my mother said she would feel more comfortable seeing a white physician, if that's okay."

A white physician. The silence that entered the room buried any other noise that was there uninvited. My head and my shoulders pulled back, no longer staring at her chart. In what seemed like forever, I found myself looking for the right words to say, trying to erase the awkward sense of wanting to apologize for not being what she requested. It was a reflex, a final reckoning within myself. It felt like I was finally being exposed for what my core daily tried to pretend it didn't acknowledge: that I am not a physician, and definitely not a white one. In that silent moment, I was reminded of how empty I felt in the OR at times, or how my skin would tighten, when someone would make a joke about a patient of color. An ER nurse once said, *"Black women have a smell to them; it's just true"*, and I, not knowing much, opted to hold my tongue to keep a peace I didn't know how to defend. I wanted to move, but I also wanted them to see my face a little longer, to see my blackness and sense my "being there." I was disappointed, but not mad; repulsed, but not resentful. I was so many things that made those few seconds feel like an hour. I no longer cared that she was sick or frail, no more than I cared that she was white. However, her words (reiterated through her son) outlined that she was bothered by my presence, a sentiment we both now shared. Standing up, I excused myself and closed the door behind me.

Dr. Lee was on the phone, pointing his index finger in the air, then eagerly waving me to come in. I sat in my usual chair, eyes fixed on the floor, my notepad empty. While walking down the hall a few moments earlier, I tried to organize what and how I should say what just occurred. Do I mention it? How do I relay what was just told to me without seeming harsh or upset? Do I smile while saying it, protecting myself from being asked if I was okay? Am I okay? Is the patient wrong for requesting to have her care managed by someone she feels more comfortable with? Was it her or her son's requests? Was it her dementia? Is this the first time such a request was made? The more I ran questions through my mind, the less time I had to answer them. Thankfully, Dr. Lee interrupted my frantic train of thoughts, which carried me into his office, with a succinct and informal question of his own.

"Okay, Jim, what'cha got?"

"Nothing," I replied. "She said she only wanted to see a white physician... so I left the room."

For the first time, I noticed he was wearing glasses today. I never noticed them before, nor any time earlier. He removed them and looked down at his crowded desk for a spot to place them, as if he was also trying to make sure he would be able to find them when needed again. Looking back at me, with his brow now furrowed more intently than it typically is while talking to his patients, he rhetorically asked, "She said... WHAT?"

Before I could answer, he stood up and left his office, with me hurriedly standing to follow behind him. The hallway leading from his office to the intake room was both narrower and higher than the other hallways in the building. The walls were a purposeful white, with painted-over scuff marks near the baseboards, which I only noticed because I would constantly look down at my notes when heading to his office to discuss a patient. Some of the scuff marks were mine; I noticed that too. The intake room was small, with only three chairs and the customary watercolor office paintings on the wall. There was a small lamp in the far corner; it flickered when the door would close too tightly. The carpet was dark brown with a dullness to it, quietly absorbing all the traffic and nervous feet shuffling it encountered throughout the day. Two patients and myself in the room was already a crowd. When Dr. Lee and I entered it that afternoon, however, it felt larger as if the moment made space for our appearance.

"Good afternoon, are you Ms. Jones?" Dr. Lee asked with a smile, nodding to acknowledge her son as well.

"Yes. Good afternoon, Doctor," she replied.

"My medical student told me that you prefer to see a white physician today", he calmly stated. "Well, we don't have any white physicians here today so I can't help you. You will have to make another appointment. Have a nice day."

He left the room, abruptly, without speaking another word. I followed in tow, accordingly, pulling the door handle behind me with a pleasing certainty that when it closed the small lamp's light would flicker. Retracing our steps down the hall, back into his office, Dr. Lee sat down in his chair and grabbed his glasses without putting them on. Turning to me, he spoke firmly.

"Well, I am sorry about that. I don't tolerate that nonsense, and you should never tolerate it either. I don't know what you are feeling right now but I want to give you the space to talk about it if you'd like. But if not, I understand as well."

"Naw, it's cool. I mean, I'm used to it," I replied, trying to diffuse the situation with my composure.

"No, it's not cool and do not ever get used it. Ever. I am a minority just like you but my 'color problems' are not your 'color problems'—we all have to get through life, but we do not have tolerate people making it hard for us. If this ever happens again, never hold your tongue. Speak up. And if no one listens, speak louder. This upsets me. I'm embarrassed that one of our patients would act in such a manner. I'm going to discuss this with the staff and remind them that this behavior is not acceptable. Again, I am sorry."

An apology wasn't needed; he did nothing wrong. However, I appreciated his sentiments and I understood why he extended them in my direction. Since that moment, I have not had any other patients make such a request, but I have felt the unassuming sting of stereotypical biases and prejudices aimed in my

vicinities. Even having a white coat with MD behind my initials wasn't enough
to avoid having my presence questioned, or ignored, during the latter stages of
my medical training. Being a "black physician" invites the curiosity of "how",
more than it welcomes the acceptance of "okay." As shocking as it is to many
physicians of color that we are 'actual' medical professionals (when compared to
what society has expected of us), it has become readily apparent that the shock
is far more evident in other racial circles. We are rarely expected, so our arrival is
not readily anticipated. Our assessments are not consistently implemented, and
our opinions are not always equally valued in workplace arenas. Oddly, we work
extremely hard to secure our place in the cradle of professional objectivity, only
to have it erased, at times, by the very subjects we have given an oath to provide
care for.

Becoming a physician is difficult. Becoming a physician while staying calm
when you are called out for being different—be it color, gender, or sexual
orientation—creates a vacuum of emptiness that is not covered well in our
medical textbooks. Many of us look for support from within and via our support
systems; however, in the actual moment, when the loudness of "-isms" invades
the room where you are told discrimination has no place, there is often no
one to lean on. There is no white coat to defend your honor, nor a nearby
door you can close that cause light bulbs to flicker. Sometimes there is a Dr.
Lee, boldly defending your integrity without hesitation. Yet, many times there
is only you, your patient or an offending coworker, and whatever response
you choose to assemble in front of the calamity of you salvaging your pride. I
remind myself, in those situations, regardless of how I feel, that my true enemy
is still the unjudging stain of human disease. I can allow my pride and anger to
consume me, thus altering the architecture of my story, or I can calmly remind
my offender that my place is not defined by whatever boxes they have opted to
put me in. That day, when my patient no longer wanted my 'color' in her room,
I opted to merely close the door, and made sure the light flickered.

no presents.

M y favorite holiday is Christmas, by far. The entire season, in my opinion, is the only time when magic truly exists. People are kinder. Traffic is easier to navigate, even when it's crowded and thicker than the lingering coldness that barely escaped November's grasp. Even more, holiday songs, which would otherwise be deemed annoying if consumed during any other time of the year, easily become the theme music behind photos and small family gatherings. Minus the drab religious imagery and chaotic extensions of Black Friday promises of the last sale being the *last sale*, nothing about the last few months of the year seems fake, or unauthentic. Hugs from relatives who owe you money don't feel deceptive. Friends, who may have slighted you earlier in the year, are forgivingly invited over to laugh off misguided deeds. The mode is lightened with a bevy of silly holiday games, eggnog, and overbaked cookies—that are more decorative than tasteful. It's a nice vibe, a welcoming one. It's a time for smiles and for re-discussing the meaning of love, as if sadness and hatred are non-humanistic emotions, existing only after December 31st and before Thanksgiving eve. Christmas is not just a holiday to me. It's a reminder that the magic of goodness is still present in the world, and in people, even if it's all just an illusion.

Our first Christmas in NJ was just that, an illusion. Arriving at my Aunt Lillie's house, one of my grandmother's nine living sisters at the time, we were greeted with the customary hugs and the African American version of yule

time cheer: food. There was food everywhere. Lima beans. Cornbre
greens with ham hocks. The aroma of cinnamon and margarine intermixing
over yams and baked ham both danced around the kitchen entrance, inviting
you to trade in your free smells for small samplings. The pies. The cakes. The
rutabaga and potatoes resting and steaming indistinguishably in smoke-stained
porcelain cookware, which reflected distorted faces of staring kids trying to
peek over the table. The rich smells of comfort and satisfied living inched over
buttery rolls and carried laughter like a generous sleigh filled with newcomers
who had just arrived. Like us. All of this was for us. My Aunt Lillie and her entire
family created a feast. They grabbed phones and made hearty calls, inviting
more and more people to come over and break bread. This was a celebration.
A pre-Christmas Eve indoor-under-a-dimly-lit-chandelier fete. A welcome back
party. The return of the anti-prodigal sister. "Hey everybody, Ella's home! Our
favorite big sister is here!"—and oh yeah, so are Joyce's kids.

Family is a very interesting word. Investigated, it essentially means "a unit,"
usually of ancestral lineage. My family unit was atypical (a grandmother, a
mother, three kids, and no pets), but this arrangement was not uncommon in
my neighborhoods. A good number of kids I knew grew up without fathers,
so someone having one felt more like the exception than the rule. My unit's
arrival in NJ was initially quite warm and receptive. The excitement in the air
surrounding our reconnection with much larger, and extended, units felt like an
unending wave. Everyone was happy to see us, asking about Joyce and when she
would arrive. The other matriarch of my unit was still on the road with Terry
and Frankie, two extensions of our unit via their affiliation with my mother.
No one asked about the extensions, though. Units are vague like that. How
they are defined is not only dynamic and multifaceted, but also varies within
the framework of religious, cultural, and social acceptances. The bigger and
much larger governing unit within my family, Ella's siblings, were deep-seated
Christians. They believed that any subunit structure within the *family* should
follow similar values and mores. Marriage was paramount, premarital existences
were not. Any unmarried couples living together were deemed to be "shacking
up", bringing disorder to the main unit and, hypocritically, dishonor to the

family name. Word got around that Ella wasn't moving Up North with just Joyce and the kids, but also with *another unit extension* (i.e., Terry). Reflexively, the loud laughter that contoured stories, memories of love, and missed time together, quickly turned into shadowed whispers and judgmental musings over cold plates of food.

Yet this is all hindsight. As a twelve-year-old, I felt the rise and fall of jubilee throughout the day, but my youthful innocence and naiveté was all too forgiving at that time. I thought the influx of quietness that matched the front door outflux of family members was merely a reflection of the early darkening of the evening sky. Everyone was probably tired. We laughed and ate a lot; hugging and telling stories can be quite exhausting. People had jobs and needed to rest; it was a Wednesday. An exceptionally cold Wednesday, my aunts noted—with no snow, just more brown grass and hard dirt. After playing outside with our cousins and saying our goodbyes, my siblings and I shuffled into my Aunt Lillie's house, unsure of what to do next.

Her house was small, but it had a warmness to it that matched the air exuding from the vents. All brick, muddy brown in color, it rested on a cul-de-sac with similarly designed houses. The yard was large and slanted downward to a rusted fence, which backed against a wooded area. The driveway rapidly ended without warning into the dried grass that kept disrupting my imagination (I struggled with the *freezing degree weather without resulting snow* for quite some time). Only there for a day, I found myself liking it—it felt like a home. Her kids were older than us. Andre, her youngest son, was in high school, as were her two younger daughters, Torri and Tonya. My Uncle Bobby, her husband and the pastor of the small church I would soon attend, worked evenings, so he left when the other family members exited under the blanket of the early night fall. Sitting around, my brain ignored my grandmother still talking over lukewarm food and sugary desserts. Instead, I started counting the remaining people in the house. One... four... six... eight. Eight people, four bedrooms, two bathrooms, and a couple couches in the living room. Joyce, two others, and my Uncle Bobby will arrive tomorrow morning.

"Where are we all going to sleep?" I whispered to myself.

Long stories are often shortened because we become numb to the particulars. Gaps are loaded with space fillers and oversized recollections of memories we carve into detailed plots. The summarized reports are shared over dinners and during midafternoon tea in small cafés. Lipstick marks on recyclable coffee cups provide the context of something indelibly alluring. Albeit unplanned, scribbled signatures on duplicated dinner receipts mentally offer the same. Our remembrances are photographic templates. We let our minds create whatever idealistic version of the past that suits our liking. If it's painful, we often circle the parts that we could tolerate. If it's a pleasant memory, then the difficult aspects are punctuated to heighten the good parts that eventually sell the story. Either/or, what is left is an abridged account; a collection of bullet points, with enough room in the margins for us to embellish a little. Yet sometimes the story has too many pieces, too many painful parts to leave out, and not enough joyful ones to make it all sound complete.

Although we arrived a few days before Christmas, and were showered with a lovely sense of anticipation, the primary pieces of our (my) new story in NJ were openly scattered before me that cold holiday morning. We finally settled into whatever spaces we could rest our heads. Jerald and I slept in Andre's room, Jessica and my grandmother found their spaces in another room in the house. Joyce, Terry, and Frankie were in a nearby motel, but arrived for Christmas breakfast and the traditional gift opening. The tree was small, and plastic, with typical ornaments that matched the dolls and other black Christmas figurines around the house, which my grandmother would praise Aunt Lillie for more than once. There were lots of gifts, wrapped nicely and some in bags. My siblings and I stood at a distance while everyone handed around packages, unsure how to feel about not hearing our names called in the beginning. When Jessica received a few items, Jerald and I let out invisible sighs because we were certain our names would be called next. And they were- twice, in fact. Two gifts each:

1. A pair of white socks

2. A packet of Lifesavers candy

As the oldest, I always understood that financially we were not as well off as others. Everyone lived in the projects in Florida, so anyone who had more (than us) was only doing a little bit better than we were. However, the celebrations were still eventful. Whether it was getting items off layaway or cutting deals with dope fiends peddling stolen goods, you could be certain that two times a year, you would receive gifts: on your birthday and on Christmas. These annual events occupied a shared duality for a kid. There was no sense of entitlement, but the expectation of receiving "something" was the highlight of our childhood. For us, these two days were not merely affiliated with getting toys and new clothes (mostly secondhand), their arrival also helped us momentarily avoid the feeling of being poor all the time. The very fabric of one's youth is centered around the notion that you mattered at least these two times per year—more than anyone else. Jerald and I felt that feeling during our birthdays that year. That winter, however, we felt something different, something unkind and cold (without the snow). This was the worst day ever, we both agreed, but this was sadly just the beginning.

The rapidity of events that followed the ending of our holiday spirit matched the swift disappearance of the aforementioned excitement of our arrival. After a week at my Aunt Lillie's house, the mumblings were starting to become more and more noticeable. Her kindness was much appreciated, but the house could not accommodate all of us for an extended period of time, so we reached out to other family members. Yet, using my Aunt Lillie's house phone this time, instead of the train station payphone, did little to alter the results. Every call Ella made started with a smile and a catching-up conversation. Then there was a long pause, then a click. Her sighs signaled their ending, followed by her (and now Joyce) thumbing through her little, black book again, hopeful someone would answer with a different answer. The warm hugs and well wishes that welcomed us a week prior became cold shoulders and, "we wish you well, but you can't stay here" occurrences. The tension was thick. It numbingly radiated the pressure they felt to our little clueless faces, whenever our eyes sought reassurance that we would have a place to go. We didn't have much there, but we left everything in Florida for what was seemed like a large piece of nothing in this new place.

Our first week of the new year was quickly ending, and somehow Ella eventually convinced a few family units to take us in (she remained at Aunt Lillie's).

My mother, Terry, and Jessica hopped around from cousin to cousin's house. Jerald and I spent a short period at my Aunt Ro's house, until we finally joined my mother in a small town called Sebring, at my cousin Junior Mack's place. His house was a lot smaller (and older) than my Aunt Lillie's, and it was often crowded with people coming and going. However, when he offered us his basement, we gladly accepted. Filled with small boxes, large broken TVs, a crooked pool table Jerald and I fancied, and a few mattresses they were no longer using, his makeshift cellar become our temporary home for a few weeks. We ignored the nauseating mildew smell and lack of carpeting, cracked open the storm window to vent the kerosene heater he let us use for heat, and made do. Since we didn't have an address, we couldn't go to school—which was fine with us. It eventually snowed, and we traded in no homework for snowball fights and snow angels. It was a brief pause in the sadness emitting from the intangible, mountainous snowfalls poorly concealing our family's recession. No later than the actual snow melting away, however, our welcoming there, also, came to an end.

More phone calls yielded connections with a few support agencies. There was a motel called The Village Inn in a nearby city (Vineland), about fifteen minutes away from Junior Mack's. It was converted into a temporary housing unit for families needing emergency accommodations. We were able to secure a room, but Joyce lied on the application about Terry tagging along, so she reminded us to keep our mouths shut, or else. The room was facing the east side of town, so we were able to enjoy the earliest glimpses of sunlight before 5 p.m. rapidly stole the rest of it away—later in the day. Two queen beds, a bathroom, and a small fridge (we kept a few perishables in) accompanied our large suitcases filled with enough clothes to last us a week or so at a time (Junior Mack let us keep the rest of our items in his basement). Jerald and I shared a bed, Joyce and Jessica shared the other. Terry slept on the floor, on a makeshift mat he created from a few tethered sheets and towels stuffed inside of a pillowcase. He noted that it was more comfortable than some of the beds he'd slept on before, even in prison. His attempt to impress us with curse-word-laden penal lore stories, however, fell flatter than the ground he was reduced to sleeping on. I couldn't make sense of why he was *still* there with us. It felt odd that he was tagging along during our struggles, as if he wanted to be around for some future expected winnings—undiscovered by the other rightful members of our unit.

And there we were. In Vineland, NJ, crammed into a small state-assisted housing situation. We were very far from the cool breezes under Florida's sunny skies, which we mistakenly traded in for windchill factors and gray clouds. Even worse, we were very close to family members who (it felt like) didn't want us around. Up North was becoming uglier by the minute. Near the end of our first month there, we had already erased any pretty long-term memories we had of the place from summertime family reunion visits. What happened to all the smiles and hugs? Earnest invites and leftover food? We went from standing in the aroma of a welcoming feast to warming up day-old KFC on a plug-in hot plate the front desk receptionist let Joyce borrow while we were there. The details have somewhat faded, but the feeling of unit-abandonment is still present. We packed up our lives haphazardly, with the hope of our parents sheltering us from the cold dangers of urban living. Then, somehow, between the blink of an eye and the silent crawl of a month's time, we were homeless—in a cold small town (where even the snow didn't stick around), living in a shelter.

A shelter. That's what it was. It wasn't an old hotel or temporary housing assistance. It wasn't a unit member's basement or a back room with an extra bed. It wasn't home. It wasn't safe. It wasn't warm or cozy, in the way the word makes you feel when you nicely describe something small. It wasn't a place you wanted to claim, nor invite people to come over and visit. It was a shelter. A place where society housed their homeless patrons to avoid having to look at them, or deal with their unfortunate realities. But to call our reality unfortunate was a stretch. We weren't displaced from our home in Florida. Certainly, we may have been behind on the rent (I wasn't privy to such information at the time) or close to being evicted, who knows, but we weren't forced to leave our southern residence. For all its drama, bad memories, and emotionally traumatizing stench, Florida and its never-ending sun never discriminated against us. It never falsely invited us over for a restful evening without ensuring we had a place to safely rest our heads. We didn't have much of a home, but we had shelter. We had an address that didn't consist of room numbers and asking front desk employees for hot plates to rewarm our food. We didn't leave paradise on the southern end of I-95, but it sure did, figuratively, feel like the exit we took off the long, northern portion of that tortuous highway was very close to hell.

Ironically, the shelter provided us with an address; thus, the state mandated we start to attend school. There was a "homeless" bus that picked up all the kids in neighboring shelters throughout the county. It was a large, embarrassing vessel, with dull, faded yellow paint exposing rusted undertones of sun-damaged metal. The Village Inn was near a busy intersection where we stood and patiently waited for its 4:15 a.m. arrival (my school started at 7:30 a.m.). We were on the first local pickup route, and when it slowed to a quick stop and the doors flung open, we shot to the back for the long, black, warmer seats near the bus's rear axles. The driver never spoke much but played R&B songs leftover from the late morning's "Lovers" playlist, which belted over the bus's rebellious transmission as it vibrated and hummed at quieter intersections. The near three-hour bus ride introduced us to groups of other *sheltered kids*, but none of them were from Florida. Some stated they moved around from shelter to shelter for years, making our transient Village Inn stop seem somewhat trivial and less burdensome. However, it still sucked—arriving at a new middle school in a rusty-brown, horribly voiced, unlabeled bus that attracted judging stares and preteen laughter. My 7:15 a.m. bus stop provided ample enough time for my classmates to get off a few jokes. Encouragingly, I would convince myself that I only had to hide my tears for fifteen minutes until the school bell rang.

Bridgeton Middle School was unlike the other three middle schools I had already attended in South Florida by my seventh-grade year. The kids there were much larger than me. They dressed in designer clothing I had never heard of before, and they were eager to make me aware of that fact. From Starter mesh pullover jackets to nubuck-colored Timberland boots, their flare for fashion matched their enthusiasm for life. Laughing with a richness that seemed to reflect an inaccessible sense of confidence, I found myself listening to their words more than they did. I was only there for a few weeks. Joyce was able to secure a small townhouse in Cedarville, a township about twenty minutes south of

Bridgeton. Once we settled in, I transferred to my fourth middle school in less than two years, Myron L. Powell Elementary. My siblings were also there because it housed students from pre-K to 8th grade. The town was in the middle of hearty farmland; half the residents were undocumented migrant workers, and the other half were whites who made up the other ninety percent of the "true" racial census, and they knew it.

The townhouse was on Main Street, which linearly connected Cedarville to all the other small towns that were south of its geographic lines. It was pastel green, with chipped yellow-and-darker-green trim around the windows. It had three bedrooms and two bathrooms—one upstairs and the other downstairs behind the kitchen. The rest of the house wasn't much to speak of; the rooms never had any personality. We didn't live there, we merely existed within its perimeter. The landlords were black, a forgivable afterthought once we moved in. I'm not sure why Ella and Joyce assumed that having black overseers would make our slave-like existence more sufferable, but it didn't. Sure, we were finally living together again (Terry eventually went back to Florida once my grand-mother's demands that "he getta job" became more demanding), but the core living situation was not much better. A few months into our stay, we got behind on the light and oil bills (a utility we didn't have to manage while down south); thus, we vacated all the upstairs rooms and huddled downstairs at nightfall around another kerosene heater we were able to secure. Thankfully, one of my second cousins, LaMark, lived in the conjoining townhome. He let us run an extension cord from his home to ours during the evening, allowing Joyce to use a newer hot plate to cook and heat water for the occasional warm bath.

That first summer offered a transient relief. No school. No oil bills. No early evenings to steal away our time away from the misery of being crowded in a cramped living room for the night, since we could stay outside and play a little longer. Ella and Joyce argued more; Jessica and Jerald echoed similar negative sentiments of "being in NJ" that I shared. However, we eventually accepted that this reality was the one we had to graciously adapt to. There was not a Plan B, nor a Plan C. We didn't have enough money to pay bills, so saving enough to go back to Florida was out of the question. The solution I conceived, as the oldest child, was to get a job. Going on thirteen but feeling like "the man," I found myself eager to go earn an honest living, even if it meant lying to myself that my vague plan made any sense at all.

Art, the owner of a local tire salvaging company, deceivingly welcomed my eagerness. He let my friend, Keaton (a kid I met at school, who was half white-half black, so was only half hated by the locals) and I lace tires in the back of tractor trailers for a meaningless wage. Our youthful ignorance allowed him to avoid any child labor issues. There was no contract, just a head nod and some sweaty, oil-stained cash handed to us when the job was completed. After Keaton got his first pay, he quit. After I got mine, I stuck around, because unlike him, I needed it. We needed it. Every dime I could muster that summer as a twelve-year-old carried us into the winter, which we all knew would be longer than the previous one. The anticipation of oil bills and other needs trumped any desire I had to keep some of the money for myself. Humbled by the fear of not being there for my family when needed, and LaMark possibly not letting us use his outlets anymore, I handed over every dollar with a sigh, and it all quickly disappeared-like magic.

The illusion of betterment never felt concrete. I thought writing about all of this would provide some sort of therapeutic outlet, but all it has done is provide more reasons to shorten long stories into brief asides. The more I type, the more I purposely leave out specific moments of struggle and awkward requests for help. The details of pain are often ignored. The feeling begs for attention, so I pay the price in full to continue moving along. Nonetheless, my reliving it and retracing the memories/associated events has stirred up emotions that I realized I never fully framed into a decent understanding.

Some things I could make sense of, but most of them I couldn't. I mean, I get why someone wouldn't want Joyce, her kids, and her energy-consuming, unemployed boyfriend sleeping in their homes during the day, eating groceries they couldn't replace, and absorbing space they couldn't afford. I get why some family members would question the decision to leave a familiar living environment for an unknown, harder-to-traverse one, without any resources or semblances of a plan. I can even make sense of the hesitation to get involved in adult issues when you have your own issues and personal troubles to address. I get the adultness of the decisions made to stay far away from our homeless situation. However, to this day, I can't fathom the ugliness of it all. I can't make sense of why one of my grandmother's "loving" sisters would take her last $500 for the purchase of a *working* vehicle, which the mechanic said was "dead before you bought it." I can't fully rationalize the disconnect other adult family members had for my siblings and I, leaving us to suffer the effects of ill-advised decisions by our parents. Joyce's kids didn't leave Florida, Joyce did. Other adults, in my extended family, may not have liked the adults in my unit, but we (the kids) bore the punishment for their disdain. There was no love extended to "those poor kids", and it felt like the reason why was because we were just some poor kids.

A childhood abandoned. No labor laws, no work hours secretly reported. The money I made was under the table, but it put food on the table, and therefore no one complained. That December, Joyce called me into the kitchen one day, while she was preparing dinner for the evening. Fully calm, but somewhat cautious, she explained that she received a $100 Family Dollar gift card from a local agency and that it was all she had for Christmas gifts. Before she could outline her plan to divide the money, I told her that I didn't want anything and that she should focus on Jerald and Jessica. Tearfully, she gave me a hug and apologized. In that moment, I realized that whatever was next for me in life wouldn't involve me being a kid anymore. I absorbed the gravity of it all. I recognized that in the span of a year, I went from being a markedly curious preteen to one of the adult members of my core family unit.

Standing there, with my broken mother in my arms, I lost the remaining aspects of my childhood a short distance from a Christmas tree (in the living room) that would soon bear gifts without my name. Yet, I found something richer and more complete that holiday season. It was something intangibly remarkable, with all the beautiful parts wrapped in a cloaked time capsule that would make sense decades later. That Christmas, I discovered that magic can only exist if you are willing to ignore that magic is just an illusion.

***

ice cold (15b)

It is basically an indoor campfire. Putting my hands closer to the kerosene heater with no Boy Scout badges to be earned, I feel its tickling warmth angrily pushing me further away as I try to get comfortable for the evening. The snow just arrived, the soft kind that leaves you wondering if it will stick around and be nosy enough to settle into a blanket. When the temperature drops a few more degrees, a confusing mixture of rain, sleet, and ice will gamble their way into the conversation for who will cast a more lasting impression. It's a dice game, but nature always wins. You can't stop its slow march or its bumbling foray under the deep darkness of December nights. All the stars disappear and make room for the entrance of a cold pallor, which is both eerily luminous and beautiful. When you step outside, however, its magnetic ugliness grips you without remorse.

Being hot is not complicated; like being cold, you can anticipate it. However, heat offers a frustration that is easily remedied: less clothes, blasting AC, or cool beverages to calm the scorching annoyance of the sun's dehydrating grasp. But when it's cold outside, there is rarely any relief other than reversing course and going back into shelter—that is, if doing so is an option. Layered clothes or boots wrapped in trash bags only temporarily shield you from the inescapable crawl of an icy chill. Cold air paradoxically burns your lungs; your words get lost in the smoky air leaping from your chapped lips and chattering teeth. Your pace slows; shivering expends energy your brain is trying to ration in exchange for a warmer core. You begin sniffling, not from crying, but rather because your body is doing everything possible to moisten the landing zone for every breath you take. However, it all hurts so you still feel like crying. The only cure for being cold is to stay far, far away from it altogether, and to stay as close as possible to the heat.

Staring out of the window from a chair pulled close to the small beige heater, the fumes radiating from its sides swirl into a poorly ventilated cloud of black smoke that blurs my view of the winter chaos. From my seat I can still see the main road, adjacent to our townhouse, and the snow is starting to layer onto it like the untouched veil of a bride. My grandmother is upstairs in her room. There is no light up there during the evening, but she is sound asleep. The walls are thin, but she is hopeful to avoid the crackling sounds being emitted from the small TV, propped on top of a makeshift stationery desk in the living room. Its missing drawers act as shelves for our VHS tapes. Most of them are videos of TV shows, copies of old sitcoms that we recorded while in Florida. Cable is not a luxury we can afford (we don't even have electricity), and the local channels are not available in our perimeter. Cedarville is in the middle of nowhere, so the only thing the antenna captures is a static halo of dust. Jerald and Jessica are on a smaller couch, in my periphery. They are ignorant of my side glances of them, bundled under a secondhand quilt made for someone else's family. I am in awe of how close they are to the same reality I am witnessing, but they are somehow utterly unmoved by the weight of how densely surreal it all feels.

We are three days into our Christmas break, and I already miss the consistent meals and scheduled predictability of school. The cafeteria food isn't the best, but it is always hot and doesn't require sharing crowded refrigerator space with roaches and spoiling milk. LaMark is graciously allowing us to still use his electricity, but we don't want to abuse his leased charity, so we only plug the fridge in during the daytime (and other appliances at night- TV, VCR, hot plate, etc.). We freeze the more perishable items and then put them in the fridge during the evening, hoping the post-sunset coldness, which inches through kitchen window crevices, will balance the dissipation of tastefulness. Hot meals are a luxury in this house; lukewarm food is the norm. Thus, three days into our miserable staycation, any joyfulness derived from not being in school is already wearing thin. Along with the freshness of warm school meals, I am also craving the overflow of snacks my eager classmates give me to be picked for my basketball team during lunch. At school I am openly respected and privately revered; the superstar eighth-grade basketball player and the only black male in all my honors classes. Young, gifted, and black; I am the anomaly. I love being there because being there meant not being here, in a cold home.

While daydreaming in the mirage of fumes thickening the air I was inhaling, Joyce asks me to turn on the hot plate and put on another pot of water. The stove that accompanies the townhouse we are renting is oil driven, which we cannot afford during the wintertime, so it is on winter break as well. One our cousins furnished us with a small single-burner hot plate, which serves as our only source of non-kerosene heat. It is generally used for boiling water for cooking, or to bathe (and also to wash our white clothes—in the same tub). It sits on the back counter, under a set of brown, badly painted cabinets that house insect and rodent droppings, along with USDA cans of various food items. Some have labels, some are just aluminum cans with dented edges. If we are lucky, the unlabeled ones have canned pork or beef, but, more often than not, the surprise is "over-salted" chopped beans or "watered-down" pastel-colored corn. We still eat it because if that is what Joyce prepares, then expecting anything else will leave us unsurprisingly disappointed.

The back counter also abuts the back room in the house, where the downstairs bathroom is located. Joyce is in there with a flashlight, fumbling in a small closet for an extension cord. Earlier today, she handwashed clothes and spread them all over the house; their wetness adding to the cold dampness that seems to invade the entire dwelling. Even with her neuropathy worsening, I never offer to help her with washing our clothes. Not because it is beneath me or because I am a male child (gender chore roles don't really exist when you're saddling the cusp of homelessness every week), but rather because I feel there is an irony buried in her completing the chore on her own. Her "sickness" and not being able to "work" because of her neuropathy partially landed us in this impoverished predicament. Yet, she is being forced to use the same disabled limbs to perform even harder labor at home than required at most of jobs. My teenage resentment of her results in a pity that is fractional. If she feels that her hovering over a half-filled bathtub while scrubbing our dirty clothes, with her numbing and atrophied fingers, makes her more of a mother, then I have no qualms whatsoever. And if any of it causes her hands to hurt a little more, then

I have no issues with helping to boil any extra water she needs—on the hot plate, on the back counter.

Moving the pot to the side, I start filling the other one I quickly grabbed from the side porch connected to the kitchen. The room isn't well insulated, so opening and closing the door makes me wonder why we don't keep food on the porch, instead of in the lukewarm fridge we store it in during the evening. There are no insects outside. The roaches and field bugs who survived the fall were inside trying to escape the cold, in exchange for the same toxic kerosene fumes we were inhaling. All in the family, there is no discrimination amongst the poor. I have actually stopped killing them because it seems like it just makes them angrier, causing them to reproduce more as if to prove their eternal affiliation. South Florida roaches, toughing out South Jersey winters. They, like myself, didn't asked to come Up North. Now they are being blamed for simply being in a place, where the same humans who brought them there no longer want them there at all.

A part of me envies their spirit, their fight. Their ability to keep showing up and surviving despite being depicted as the epitome of filth. Poisoned and homes fumigated with Raid, their scattering for a place to not be bothered is instinctual. There is no existential purpose in their efforts. However, they are deemed vermin, not by design, but rather because someone, someday, said their presence is not welcomed and is difficult to control. They are practically harmless insects, with hundreds of millions of years, of survival, etched into their small collection of DNA strands. They have proved themselves more viable and capable of withstanding ice ages and cataclysmic world events, which would have decimated their human counterparts. But their existence reflects social norms that have gone astray; puddled with the poor, the unclean, and the untouchables. Their efforts of merely performing their genetic obligation to reproduce and endure is unsuitable. Not because they bring any significant harm, but because of their subhuman form. They are, since no one likes them, unwanted and disgusting. Displaced. Problematic. Burdensome. Not homeless, but definitely not welcomed into any homes. Yet here they are, existing, multiplying, and somehow surviving a second winter in Up North with us- at home.

"Jimmy! Damn!" Joyce yells as she pushes me away from the pot.

My transient loss of focus results in the pot overflowing and spilling all over the floor. Joyce quickly uses a dirty towel from the bathroom to soak up the water before if seeps into the rotting lower portions of the counter cabinets, which our landlord was already trying to charge us for damaging. I quickly help; apologetic in my stares, but upset with myself in the moment for creating a problem. A new problem. A small one, but certainly one we don't need. We are already months behind on the rent. Another ding on our tab will only lead to more gloom and shattered promise that the new year will be much of the same. As I try to shove the towel against the base of the cabinet, my knuckles start to scrap against the rough edges of the wilted vinyl tiles, causing them to bleed. Unaware of my injuries, I keep forcefully pushing the towel, harder and harder, until Joyce notices the blood starting to stain the white threads.

"Jimmy! You're bleeding. Stop! Stop!" she screams, grabbing my arms and inspecting my hands and then looking up to notice that I'm crying. "Why are you crying? Does it hurt? What's wrong, baby?"

Not knowing what to do or say, I freeze. I am not in pain, but the tears are racing down my cheeks as a wave of anger, and frustration, and sadness run throughout my entire existence. Lips pursed, I begin breathing heavily through my nose, while trying to hold together all the quieted angst that has been building inside of me for years and years. Then she, for the second time in weeks, hugs me. And for the first time, in a very long time, I let go. I let go of all the pressure of being the best kid and the smartest student. I let go of all the fake smiles and "I'm okay" lies I mutter whenever asked how I am feeling. I let go of the fear of being a boy who is being called to be *the man*, a role I don't really want because I still feel like a boy. I let go of Big Jimmy leaving and Poochie not caring. I let go of putting Jerald and Jessica first all the time, of feeling like my feelings are not worthy enough of being entitled or appreciated. In that moment, I feel free. I sit there, on the floor, leaning into my mother's arms, crying on her shoulders, and let myself be a thirteen-year-old kid who just needs a hug.

Hours later, I lie in my bed upstairs, embracing the thick darkness that has an almost poetic calm to it. My injured hand behind my head, I feel my knuckles still burning but starting to soothe from the coolness under my pillow. The window curtain is closed but angled enough to the side that portions of moonlight, and the light it reflects from the snowy ground, creates a thin vertical line that abruptly disappears before it reaches the ceiling. Tears drying on my face, I stare at the trace of light, wondering how it feels having traveled millions of miles away, from distant galaxies, only to be reduced to a small line on the corner of a wall in my room. A room with no electricity; no posters of foreign cars or childhood sports heroes. A room with two sweat-stained twin beds that are footnoted by two large cardboard boxes of old clothes. It doesn't belong there, a celestial creation reduced to the oblivion of my imagination. This rich ray of energy is now being examined in a poor boy's room, contrasting the fallacy of human life: You can be the best and most powerful thing ever, but in the wrong location you can look completely out of line.

I feel lost and faraway from some other life I failed to encounter, mistakenly landing in some boy's room, at an address I must have gotten wrong. My inner brilliance feels displaced, sullied by blood-soaked towels I used to absorb all the wrong things I didn't cause. I feel special, and different. I knew I have a purpose, but I am becoming more and more afraid of accepting that this is it—a boy destined to lose his chance at being a boy. I am not whining or crying over spilled milk; we don't have any milk to spill. And whatever milk we have is always about to spoil, so no one cares if it spills anyway. Yet I can't manage to figure out how any of this is my fault, or why it also becoming my problem.

Hours earlier, I was downstairs, crying in my mother's arms and I didn't want to leave. Not because I needed her love, but rather because I needed to not be her provider or her replacement for failed men in her life. I needed to know that although I am not the only child in her world, I am still a child that matters. Not a young adult. Not a coworker or a co-bill payer. Not her "little big guy" whose problems are well managed with head nods and the silent hope that I am old enough to understand. I am not an answer to a prayer, nor a handful of school money from a summer job used to catch up on the rent, but a child. Her child. Her light beam from far, far away, that somehow stopped illuminating whatever room he was in before he reached his ceiling. I wanted her to know that just because I am not showing how much I hated our existence, it doesn't mean that I fail to grasp just how deeply I don't love it.

I wake up hours later, with the room filled with morning sun and the aroma of bacon being cooked downstairs. I look at my hand and notice the dried blood covering the patchy areas of open skin. It doesn't hurt, but seeing it again reminds me of the pain. I jump up and head downstairs. The living room is empty except for the stench of kerosene smoke that permanently lingers. Joyce is in the kitchen, cooking and talking to Ella. Before heading across the room to nosily see what else is accompanying the fumes that are capturing my attention, I turn and look at the window I was staring out of the night before, hoping to see my siblings.

The veil covering the road from last night has lifted, replaced by mud-stained tire tracks, with its virgin whiteness plowed to the side into piles of graying ice. I head to the front door, and before I open it, I see a small baby roach, scurrying alongside a crack in the wall, right above the door frame. It pauses with its antenna rapidly scanning the air, trying to figure out what to do next. I watch as it hurries toward the area opposite the crack, into an open space of the wall, exposed and vulnerable in its effort to traverse the room. Halfway into its trek, it stops again, scans the air, and remains out in the open, peacefully still. After staring at it for a few more seconds, I smile and open the door, putting my fingers out to gauge how cold it is.

"Sheesh," I whisper, pulling my hand away from the cold stinging air, as I rub it against my other hand with bruised knuckles—blowing into them both for a little heat.

interlude.

bumblebees

my little bumblebees
big box... fort... building
flower chasing
architext-ure of your hair
keeps me smiling.
the air...
blows easier when you're outside.
small glimpses of ... my nose
and your mother's eyes
a fraction of our skin tone
buried under the expectations
of a cold world I hope
the sun protects you from.
but if doesn't... don't
don't be surprised.
there is no place here for black girls.
that's why I slave so you don't have to,
graveyard shifts, stealing time away

from my
effort to avoid... the inevitability of
a grave.
staring at moons that are half blue,
half the opposite of me
fully exposed, I'm...
hopeful that everything I lose is cool
as long as I have you.
bumbling... and... being... and
unraveling the mystery of imagination
and the quiet imprisonment of youth that is
still quite loud... and freeing.
my sidewalk now has flowers
blossoming divinity and tickling
pollen spores that your body
can't absorb without... tears
preventing you from seeing.
I explain that life is funny that way.
some of the things you will love
won't love you back
some of the joys you jack and jill
nursery rhyme about
won't give you jack.
and sometimes you won't like
how that feels...
but still pick flowers.
still go outside and bumble-
be(e) expressive when you win
and figure it all out...
but still laugh when you fall,
and realize everything you held close
to you... you somehow managed

to fumble.
still stay in whatever element
of your being
that brings you excitement about yourself
yet keeps you standing close enough
to a calm reality
that reminds you to stay humble.
be... whatever you want to be...
but always be my little bumblebees.
rumbling through flowers.
yeah... rumble, young girls rumble.

justa spot.

B ridgeton was livelier back in the 1990s. Seated in the northwest corner of Cumberland County, it was the closest "larger-small" city we had access to via Cedarville's main roads. At first glance, the three-story, old Victorian homes lining its single-laned roads gave it a middle-class regal appearance. In reality, they were all transitioned into multi-housing units for lower-wage families. Unlike Cedarville, Bridgeton was colorful. Not just blossoming violets and dogwood lilies in the shadow of parallel parked cars, but people colors—especially black people colors.

The aura of soulful enrichment nearly smacked you in the face whenever you entered the city limits. From loud music radiating out of car speakers to kids shouting while dodging the stares of onlooking porch-sitters, the locals were filled with a stereotypical flare of black awesomeness. Whenever we could afford to travel there to see family or go to the grocery store (there were none in Cedarville), my eyes would stick themselves to all the skin tones that reminded me of Florida. Light skins and dark skins, all shades of blackness, filling sidewalks and street corners like Spike Lee movie extras. Bridgeton made me miss being back home; it was missing the constant sunshine and hot-sanded beach shores. The more we visited, the more it sunk in that I had to get used to these sporadic eye catches of colors because this was home now. South Jersey. Cumberland County. The roads that connected Bridgeton to Cedarville. The pastel green house with the ever-present mementos, which reminded us that although we had a place to sleep, we were very much still poor—and still felt very close to being homeless.

The hardest part of homelessness is not the "not having a house" part, but rather the lingering fear that at any moment you might not have a place to go. We shuffled between extreme poverty states our first two years in NJ. Rent was usually late, bills were always overdue, and our neighbors were tiring of our awkwardly inconvenient requests for all sorts of items—sugar, milk, rides to the grocery store, and even, audaciously, money before paying back the cash lent to us weeks prior. It was dauntingly pathetic; we were perpetually on the cusp of utter disaster, but we were numb to it. The laughs at school. The judging comments about what we should and shouldn't do to make our situation better. The epic mound of failed attempts to seem normal, and not be afraid that every knock at the door was a bill collector or served notice for an uncollected bill. I found myself becoming more the "man of the house," so these worries shifted onto my shoulders as well. After the bustling chaotic nuances of teenage school life, my homework was making sure that everything at the home worked. And whenever something remained irreparably broken, its failed usefulness stuck around and reminded us that we shared a similar existence.

Cedarville, for all its smalltown charm, was not so pretty when it came to a social existence. There was a hint of racial undertones everywhere we went; corner store and post office visits were accompanied by uncomfortable stares and tightened lips. We were never bullied, though. My friends and I muscled together in packs, Jerald and Huggy (another friend I met who shared in our struggle) near the front, the rest of us casually in the back with arms crossed and eyes gleaming with the youthful exuberance of young black boys realizing their presence alone invited fear. The fights came and went, as did our concern for the embarrassment of losing. Life, at least for Jerald and me, was already a series of losses; another one did little to deter us from a battle. Be it sports, swimming races in old cranberry factory lakes, snapping matches at school, or staring contests with little old white ladies in local post office atriums, we were not afraid of the town's contempt of our growing acceptance that we were assertively "the poor." Our black stains matched the dilated pupils of their off-white glances, and our reflection in their eyes were subtle tokens that these young token negroes truly didn't care.

I had the privilege, however, of leaving Cedarville's backwoods harshness on a regular basis once I graduated from its highest available academic platform: I went to high school. The nearest one was in Bridgeton, with one bus serving all the southern towns requiring its scholastic tutelage. Although its hallways and cafeterias carried the same prototypical pubescent energy, which was also wrapped in its team-spirited affirmations, my vibrating imagination and desire to escape hell (my home life) welcomed the amnesty it relayed. People watching never failed to entertain; the cool kids and pretty girls who walked by wearing football player jerseys offered proof that superiority was a limited commodity. I faded in the background of their noise, shy and careful not to draw attention to myself, but I was curiously intrigued by their slang and "New Jersey" flash. My introduction to where I fit in the social hierarchy, and didn't, was swift; a line was drawn that I never crossed nor entertained questioning out loud. Smelling like the kerosene heat fumes used to speed dry clothes my mother washed on her hands, I was both aware and unaware as to why I had so few friends. Those I did have were close enough to deem reliable; the others that I lost were not expected to stick around anyway. I didn't care. I was not at *that house* when I was there, and not being at *that house* felt alive.

My saving grace, and eventual invitation to the acceptable side of reality, came that fall when basketball season arrived. If there was ever an equalizer of all the things humans have used to separate each other into boxes that made very little sense, then sports arguably topped that list. Physical attributes aside, you'd be hard-pressed to find a more unifying and difference-erasing activity than a simple game of any kind. Perfection is never attainable in said arenas, but desired. Athletes push themselves past mental and physical limits in order to gain competitive edges that sometimes border insanity, creating awe in the process. When these efforts are matched in elevated intensity with others who share similar team-oriented goals, any differences that isolated them before are merely addendums after commencement whistles are blown. Add the intoxicating allure of bottled teenage machismo to that mix, and you are left with a battlefield that can either strip away a young man's confidence or, as in my case, ignite a fire that is more intense than the kerosene heater that dried my clothes.

Basketball was life for me back then. I lived it. I consumed it. I thought about it ceaselessly, dreamed about it when I had nothing else to invite to my dreams. The group of positives in my world, at the time, was that I was very good at three things: lying about how much I was bothered by our impoverished existence, performing well at school, and playing basketball. The former two required a sizeable amount of effort, the latter came easy and was reflexive. I could walk on any court, in any town, and hold my own. I was quick but not hurried, calm but unrelenting. Whenever I sensed a weaker opponent, my gentle demeanor kindly took a seat on the bench and let my aggression create highlight reels that eventually caught the attention of nearby competitors. When they arrived, they lost. And the very few who won, still offered careful warnings to anyone else awaiting their turn to play the tall skinny kid from Cedarville they called "Moss." I took this same energy and deep-seated eagerness to prove my worth to my high school basketball tryouts during my freshman year. I made the team, and I was also suiting up for varsity games by the end of the first month. For the first time in my life, I was being noticed. My veil was sliding back, my self-confidence was beginning to flourish, my escapes from home were becoming consistently enjoyable, and then my reality reared its ugly head.

Cedarville was a solid twenty to twenty-five-minute bus ride from Bridgeton. The one bus that took all the southern smalltown kids back and forth to school made that route only once, so if you missed it you had to catch the "late bus" back home, which left at 7:30 p.m. This allowed time for athletes to play their perspective sports and still have safe transportation home afterward. The JV games and other sports typically ended around 7p.m. Students would shower, joke around until the late buses arrived and made their rounds, and then head home—stretched out on long seats that could barely fit their egos or hold their endless late evening jubilation. After my games, I was afraid to miss my only ride home, so I skipped the showers and waited outside for the bus to arrive. Keaton played JV as well, so his company was reliable and equally entertaining. We stared at cheerleaders and tried to avoid any of their varsity boyfriends catching us stealing glances. This routine sufficed for the first few weeks of the basketball season. Then one day, after practice, our head coach, Coach K, looked at me said, "Hey, Moss. Next game, Pleasantville. I want you to suit for Varsity."

"Yes, sir. Thank you," I confidently replied.

Pleasantville was our "no-so-pleasant" cross-state rival. It wasn't much of a rivalry at the time, though. They were colossal. Towering in height (their shortest player was taller than our tallest player), dripping in ability and athleticism that equal some Division III college teams. They were primed for state playoffs, and potentially a national championship as well. With a few players that probably could have turned pro if they didn't live in Pleasantville, the mere idea of gracing the court against them would strike fear in most high school athletes. They were bigger and better than us, but we were fearless. We had top-notch local legends who were multisport Gods walking our hallways with Adonis-like auras. Robby Tukes. Rick Mosely. Damon Powell. Terrance Jackson. Mo Brown. The list of names was endless; all of them were gifted and capable of beating almost any team in the state that year—except Pleasantville.

They knew it. We knew it. Our coaches and fans knew it, and more noticeably, Pleasantville knew it too. We were both undefeated at that time; numbers 1 and 2 in our shared conference. The newspapers tried to hype the game up as one for the ages. However, the hype was more of everyone hoping to capture a glimpse of the Goliaths, who were soon to arrive to play against our hometown collection of Davids. The eagerness of my first varsity game, which I was most likely only going to play in if, and when, the score got out of hand, didn't evoke any fear inside of me. Playing basketball against anyone, regardless of their talent level, was the least of my concerns. My only thought, and immediate apprehension, after my initial excitement waned from my name being called, was that the game ended at 10 p.m.

There were no varsity basketball players who lived in Cedarville at the time, so late-night games were never a thought. The school relied on family members to pick their kids up afterward, which was both rational and expected. My family, unfortunately, did not have the means, nor the vehicle, to ensure a late evening ride home for me. We were barely able to obtain transportation to grocery stores during the first of the month—when food stamps were issued. Doing so required a portion of our stamps or money we didn't have. After the Pleasantville annihilation (they beat us 127 to 43), I played in a few more varsity games. The out-of-town games, however, pushed our team's arrival time back to school close to12 a.m. With only a handful of quarters and numerous broken IOU promises, it was becoming difficult to acquire late evening rides home. Some nights, I would walk to a local family member's house, my cousin Shawn, crash on the couch and re-wear my clothes to school the next day. Some nights I would convince a friend's parent, or a coach, to give me a ride, but that soon became burdensome. And when all my options were exhausted, and my pride (and fear of rejection) wouldn't let me ask another soul for another favor, I implemented what eventually became my typical plan. Quickly heading out of the locker room backdoor, to avoid the pitiful stares of teammates/coaches, I'd tuck my pride into my fleece and head down to the local 7-Eleven store—to my spot.

That's all it was, just a spot. A half mile from the high school, on the corner of Broad and Lawrence streets, the twenty-four-hour 7-Eleven was the closest, well-lit facility open late enough for me to stand and wait for a potential ride. Loitering under a *No Loitering* sign, next to a payphone, with the cold air stabbing through the holes of my navy-blue fleece, my presence was both noticeable and conveniently forgetful. Patrons who were just at the games would wave and state their customary "You good?", to which I would lie and reply that I was just waiting for my ride. Nervously jingling my last few quarters in my pocket, I would watch as the steam from my deep sighs evaporated along with any hope I had of someone answering my call. Voicemails were dangerous thieves. I needed a person to talk to, not money-stealing machines that offered no promise of help. Hungry. Broke. Frozen. Scared. I would stand there for hours on end, begging my fatigued legs to stay up and keep me company for a little while longer.

Too naïve to realize just how dangerous my being there was, I found myself opting to sketch moments in my life where I survived being in similar spots. Earlier emotional childhood traumas. Domestic violence observances. Poorly lit homeless shelter bedrooms, with the invading stench of soured wet clothes from being left in laundry bags too long. I thought about when I sat on five-gallon buckets, between the driver and passenger seats in a tractor trailer, next to my chain-smoking superiors. I thought about how me being *"twelve going on whatever age they told the law"* did little to disrupt their fantastical tales of prostitution excursions and weekend drug binges. I thought about Joyce complaining of her worsening neuropathy, as she washed our clothes with lukewarm water filled bathtubs that were never clean—nor fully drained. I thought of any and everything that would steal my mind away from the cold that was robbing me of time and pocket change by the second. Ella's never-ending faith in a God that I hardly noticed. My sibling's impatient anticipation of a faded sense of betterment. Joyce's questionable reliance on the notion that somehow a "disability check" would come and save us from oblivion. I traded my spot for whatever else was foolish enough to take its place in my mind. There were hardly any takers, though, so, more often than not, I just stood there—in my spot, hopeful it would all just pass.

Life wasn't much more different moving forward: more spots, with more drama interjected into the comedy that was becoming my young existence. I learned that bad times were temporary, bad jobs were a norm (that following summer I worked on a farm with similar results: more money, more bills), and bad feelings about my situation only mattered if I allowed them to. Maturation. Acceptance. Tolerance. I started to make sense of the transient states that shadowed my life back then. The more it all started to fit into the scheme of things, the less I liked it. Teenage life felt like preteen and childhood life, just with more alone time and fewer reasons to believe that things would get better. I learned to drive. I started to notice women more. I reached my zenith in basketball, with my injuries overcoming the pain of not having a lot of family support. Ella and Joyce never watched any of my games, partially because they didn't have transportation and because Joyce was "actually" becoming quite ill. The idea of college only entered my train of thought when my academic train docked into my eleventh-grade honors English class, with Mr. Price. One day, he asked us all to write a letter to one teacher who inspired us the most, who really made a huge difference in our lives. I smiled because, for the first time in high school, something easy was given to me. I knew exactly what I would write and exactly who I would write about; the one person who brought a true sense of color into my otherwise colorless teenage life: my ninth-grade art teacher, Ms. Kenny.

homecoming.

The Florida State College of Medicine Auditorium, now named Durell Peaden Auditorium, after the late Florida state senator and physician who assisted in helping to establish the school's existence in 2000, was only partially filled when I took my seat in the back. I was sitting there, with my new backpack and laptop, furnished to us by the school, eagerly awaiting my first "doctor" lecture. It was mid-June, 2006, four months after receiving my formal notice that I was accepted into FSU COM's graduating class of 2010. The more I repeated the word "doctor" to myself, the more surreal it felt. *Doctor.* I am in medical school about to start my journey toward becoming a medical *Doctor.*

My acceptance into medical school—in of itself—was a milestone I'll never forget. The vibration of the phone conversation with Mrs. Elaine G., stating I've been accepted, still rings within my soul, as does the image of Ella, who resided with me at the time, jumping up and down in the kitchen on arthritic knees when I told her "I got in." There were doubts, doubters, and many reasons for my superiors to hit pause buttons and remind me that I was stepping into an arena that wasn't suited for my kind. Yet there was also an aura of "it's about time" that I couldn't shake, as if all my good deeds were finally catching up to my bad luck. That year was tough for me. On the tail ends of a divorce, and having moved Ella in with me because of her failing health, I found myself, forever the altruistic provider and caretaker, actually doing something for me for once:

furthering my future. I wasn't just taking classes anymore and no longer the butt of "he's still in school?" jokes. I was building a career, carving a path I felt was starting to prove that all my efforts to roll the dice on Jimmy Moss weren't in vain. There was a jubilee in my voice, my smile felt assured and authentic. This was my time, my shot, and my chance. I wasn't trying to become a doctor, I was shortly about to become one. The mere idea was next-level exciting, but that excitement faded into a swift and roaring wave of intimidation, because like, "How?"

How did I get here? How did I convince someone, well, anyone, that I, of so little educational pedigree, have what it takes to embark on the scholastic equivalent of climbing Mt Everest with no equipment? Becoming a physician sounds nice, but talking to my fellow classmates prior to our first lecture immediately reminded me that I was out of my league. These were not just smart kids; they were the smartest kids. Young, bright, and frighteningly unaware of how intelligent they were, I casually smiled and listened to their stories of academic lineage and ancestral connections to higher-level education. They were bred for this moment, groomed since young childhood to not only dream about reaching the pinnacle of success, but to make it look easy as well. While I was hoping the lights would turn on when I hit electric switches at home as a kid, many of them were in science camps learning about electricity. This was a different league, a different tier of students. Their wide eyes and constant head turning, looking around at their fellow competitors, was the only sign that their mental arsenal held any residue of nervousness. They were elite and understood it. I did too. So, when that first day arrived, I was sure to sit in the back- way in the back.

Our buzzing chatter was quickly halted when Dr. Alma Littles entered the room. A small-figured, but rather imposing, woman, her dark skin matched the dilated pupils staring at her while she stood at the podium. She introduced herself as Associate Dean of Medical Affairs, and then outlined the school's mission statement and expectations for everyone in attendance—including the kids in the back. Smiling as she verbalized the tenets of medical education, the settled poise in her pulled me in and I hung onto every word. Every inflection in her speech guided my intrigue and desire to believe every ounce of her truth. And then she uttered the words that would stay with me even to this day:

"This is not just a career choice you have chosen... this is a calling", she proclaimed while looking at the sea of young faces trying not to move or lose eye contact with her.

A calling. Those words alone erased any prior doubt I had about my being there. Because she was right; we were all called to this field. Regardless of where we were before that moment, life found a way to filter us all into that one school, in that one room, listening to one woman tell us that from here on out, what made us different also made us all quite the same. The more I listened, the more I accepted my seat at the table. I quickly looked around and instead of paying attention to everyone else, I focused on my surroundings—my seat, my presence. I belonged there. I was a good fit. No one gave me this position; they merely opened the door and provided me with an avenue to reach my newest goal in life: to become a physician. Whatever happened before the summer of 2006 already happened. She reminded my classmates and I of an old quote she once read:

"Your childhood may have been bad or difficult, but it's over. Now starts the next chapter of your book."

Our lecture ended with a barrage of thoughts and elation. Whatever she wanted to accomplish within us in the spirit of inspiration, she did. Those first six months were very difficult and life consuming, but my classmates and I made it through. All the studying, all the tests, it was all coming together. We may not have felt like physicians during our first year of medical training, but the sense of purpose that inched into our core was apparent in our conversations and hallway laughter between classes. From white coat ceremonies to encountering "real" patients after practicing our exam skills on mock ones, we were beginning to pick up on "the calling" Dr. Littles spoke of months earlier. That winter break, nonetheless, was a welcome escape. Medical school had awakened us to a new adulthood, but the prospects of going home again for the first time as "student doctors" offered a childlike getaway no one was willing to decline.

Despite the joy of having Ella with me for the past year, as she and I both were trying to recover (her from medical issues, myself from the emotional letdown of a divorce), she eventually moved back to NJ to be closer to Joyce. Her move to Florida always felt transient, though. The bond between her and Joyce was beyond the confines of geographical boundaries. Joyce was better at being her daughter than she was at being our mother. Ella regretted that the difference was noticeable, but she could do little to get that point across. But I missed them both; thus, my heading home was both a mental vacation and a homecoming, for us all. My only hesitation stemmed from financial restraints. Not simply because of the misfortunes of living loan check to loan check as a medical student, but because years earlier, Joyce had opened a series of credit cards in my name, and never paid the bill.

They didn't check credit scores for graduate school, and for that I was thankful. The admission committee was already leery of admitting a nontraditional student who was taking care of his ailing grandmother. Their concerns were warranted. The stress of becoming a physician, multiplied by balancing the medical needs of an aging relative, is enough to break the firmest of spirits. Add on mounting debt from school and a low credit score stemming from identity fraud by another relative (my mother), and the beaming hopes found in the underpinnings of my strong GPA would have quickly started to fade into a cloud of weakening support. I was not in the room when my admissions case was discussed, but I heard about the doubters and naysayers. Luckily, they didn't have my credit score in hand, and, thankfully, I never had to press charges on Poochie. I denied recognizing the signature of the perpetrator when I was furnished the credit card receipts, but when I saw my mother's distinctive *J*, it nearly floored me. How could she? Why would she? I cried on the inside, saving my tears for when I was alone in the car. She denied it was her signature when I called, and in that moment, I instantly realized that my relationship with her was dead. All I could see was more pain, all I could feel was more resentment. She and I didn't speak for years after that encounter. Until Ella got sick.

Her doctor said her heart was failing because of a bad rhythm, yet I blamed it on her having to be the heartbeat of an entire team for four-plus decades—mostly alone. She had atrial fibrillation, which causes the top part of the heart to beat so erratically that it doesn't communicate well with the bottom part of the heart. It was difficult to control. Still trying to finish my premed studies, I was unable to offer any insight at the time. However, the few doctors I shadowed offered to see her if she moved in with me. Upon her arrival, a few medication changes, and some stress-free Florida sun, fixed things in a matter of weeks. She was exercising, eating healthy, and finally able to rest. I literally saw years of drama and disappointment empty from the bags under her eyes, only to watch them refill again when Joyce called her saying she wanted her to come back home.

My arrival in NJ that winter was quite eventful; I was home for the first time since "getting into medical school" and there was a celebratory tone lining the phone calls and welcoming hugs extended in my direction. I visited all the aunts and cousins I could, finding rest only between pauses to eat. I had no agenda, but I made the customary rounds to relatives who had prayers to give, stories to tell, and food that, to this day, I blame for weight gains I have yet to lose. Once those obligations were fulfilled, I hooked up with Keaton and my other childhood friends. To the world, I was the future doctor; to my friends, I was just "Moss." I loved the freedom of not having to be on my guard the entire time. Medical school created such a high aura of professionalism around us that we closed our juvenile Facebook accounts. We traded in photos of us with red Solo cups for those of us studying with red eyes straining to find a place to land our focus amid the blur of fatigue. I went from an encyclopedic zombie to a rested new soul. I was home, I was at peace, I was loved and equally adored. Even Joyce and I made peaceful attempts to hide our principal life indifferences. Her, smiling and pretending nothing occurred, me, not caring because this moment was finally about me.

Before I headed back to Florida, I had one last stop on my list of "people to see." Bridgeton High School was nearing their winter break. I called and was thankful that a few staff members from my days roaming the halls were still there and remembered me. Walking into the office felt surreal. The students all seemed smaller and younger than those from my cohort. Nothing changed much about the main office, except some of the faces. The same posters lined the walls, and the same awkward feeling of dread still loomed when I walked through the doors (although I never went there for bad reasons and was well beyond the stage of any disciplinary threats). A school office is still a school office, though; you walk in quietly and you wait your turn to state your case. Even though I was there for a cordial visit, I signed my name on the guests list, like everyone else, and sat in one of the undersized seats that squeaked when I lowered myself into it—like everyone else. Once my "name was called," the thick wave of aired tension subsided. Warm smiles entered my space, followed by staff showing me off to other staff members who never met me before. I hugged guidance counselors and bashfully avoided their praises. The feeling was nice, but somewhat isolated. Some of the people I met were new, and many of the people I wanted to see were no longer there. I asked about various teachers and, in particular, I asked if Ms. Kenny was currently present. I was told she was, and that her class was still down the same hall and still in the same room.

I met Ms. Kenny during my ninth-grade year. She taught Introduction to Art, a subject I was fondly interested in for reasons beyond my artistic abilities. My friends, Keaton and Ricky, were in her class, as well; the former being the better artist and the latter just wanting to be around his other friends. Her class was small but had its own unique ambiance that matched her style. She wore long pearls and fanciful costume jewelry that always coordinated well with her outfits and eyeglass frames. Soft spoken and articulate, her demeanor suited her teaching disposition, as she never raised her voice to be heard and never tolerated anyone else raising theirs. Her principles were simple: respect the past (i.e., art history) and build the future. She taught us the basic artistic techniques, such as rendering and contouring, and pushed us to not simply mirror what we saw through our works, but rather what we felt. Our introduction to classical artists was filled with vibrant stories of their humanistic flaws. Van Gogh's isolated mental illnesses; the womanizing dealings of Diego Rivera. We learned to appreciate their greatness via understanding their imperfections. Art reflected life in her classroom, but on occasion a few students reflected their true colors instead.

It was an easy class if you wanted it to be easy. The work was subjective. No one could tell you that your pieces were not "good"; you were merely judged on effort. If you tried, you got a passing grade. Some students took the class for those reasons, faking their way through the semester for a spot filler on their report cards. Ms. Kenny knew this; she left them in their inactive spaces and focused on the students who wanted to learn, such as myself. One day, during a movie about Renaissance painters, I found myself fascinated by a few kids in the back who were joking around. We all got detention for our tactless disturbances, and, after class, Ms. Kenny pulled me to the side.

"Jimmy, what's going on?" she asked. "That type of behavior is unlike you."

"I'm sorry. I was laughing at their jokes and I don't know... I apologize." I was afraid that my detention would get back to my high school basketball coach, Coach Kates.

"You're a good student. I have heard nothing but great things about you. Don't waste it all away being a class clown. If you want to joke around, fine... be a jokester. But do it on your own time. Not my time. You have a lot of promise, and the biggest problem you will encounter is other people who won't care about your promise or theirs. Just be more observant. If you don't know who is for you or against you, just sit back... and pay attention. Look around. Time will reveal the truth about everyone in your life. Not just here... but in every situation."

I stood there motionless, unsure of what to say or do next. Her words still trying to find place in my spirit, she further settled the quietness inching its way in between with a deal: If I promised to be more observant of my immediate environment, she would remove my detention. That same week, the students I was joking around with were expelled from school, one for bringing weapons to another classroom and the other for fighting on the bus. The days following their absence, Ms. Kenny called their names during roll call, echoing the silence of nothingness that followed with a calm glance in my direction. She didn't have to say a word; the point she was making was understood. In fact, I carried her advice with me throughout my remaining time in high school. From so-called neighborhood friends to family members who never had my best interests at hand, I learned that sitting back and simply allowing people to reveal their true intentions usually provided answers their words failed to outline. Patience. The key to understanding the direction of any situation or circumstance, be it an unfinished 17th-century classical painting or a decision to go joyriding with a group of "friends" who may have acquired the vehicle via illegitimate means, is letting time sort out the details.

I left her class with a renewed sense of self, with many core life lessons not bulleted in the syllabus. A couple years later, I penned her a letter while in Mr. Price's Honors English class, and it sparked a bond between she and I that lasted outside of classroom walls. When she learned that my family was on hard times, she pulled some strings with her sister to secure me a summer job delivering lunches to other poor kids around the county. I was able to use the money I earned to get Joyce a washing machine, catch up on bills, and even purchase school clothes for my siblings and myself. She and her family gave me a chance to provide for mine, and my letter stated my thanks and how much she improved the quality of my life.

Knocking on her classroom door, I nervously rounded the narrow entrance, catching her off guard as she was in her typical stance—waving her jewelry-soaked hands across the space in front of her and her students. When she turned to me, she gasped and placed her hands over of her mouth. Her face and voice, now capturing the essence of time, still held a memorable tone of kindness. We embraced, as she cried and repeatedly patted my back, saying how proud she was of me when she heard I got into medical school. Her students sat quietly in the audience of our front stage homecoming scene; no large food platters or sensational prayers were exchanged during this one though. I thanked her and spoke to her class briefly about all that I learned from her, and I encouraged them to stay focused and follow their dreams.

During question-and-answer time, one student asked, "Are you the guy from the letter?"

"The letter?" I replied.

I turned to Ms. Kenny as she dried the tears that were beginning to disrupt her eyeliner, then reached into the top drawer of her desk and pulled out a folder labeled "Jimmy." Inside of it was a laminated copy of the letter I wrote to her, nine years earlier. She handed it to me and said, "There are days when I don't feel like being a teacher anymore, when it seems like no one is listening or cares about the lessons or stories. There were years when I was sure they would be my last. Retirement seemed more definite and just made more sense than to keep coming back. But then I look at this letter and remind myself that there just might be another Jimmy Moss in my class; that there might be a student who I impact to the point that they write me another letter like this. THIS letter, Jimmy, is why I became a teacher... and THIS letter... is why I still do it."

With tears now in my eyes, I hugged her again and shared that her selfless efforts on my behalf will always be at the core of who I am. I promised to visit whenever I was in town, and the next few times I did come home, I visited her room and we talked about the letter. The words became blurred over time, but the message was the same: thankfulness. The spark she provided etched into my soul the notion that the difference between confidence and arrogance is often your audience. Defining your environment, however, starts with stepping back and learning to observe how individuals move within your vicinity.

In medicine, time and patience will eventually provide the answer to a problem. Sometimes that answer is too far behind the rumbling tide of disease and is unable to stop the arriving wave of death. Yet, in our efforts, we can convey compassion and somehow relay to our patients that the masterpiece of their well-being may be flawed, but it still holds value. As physicians, we are called to be wellness liaisons. We serve as a bridge between how our patients feel about their morbidities and the reality of their mortality. We hold the promise that our observations carry an element of truth and enlightenment, and that what we see, in time, will eventually make sense. How we deliver this sentiment, as Dr. Littles once noted, is sometimes called the art of medicine, and I am grateful I learned its principles at an early age via my dealings with Ms. Kenny, when she taught me about beauty and subtleties in the art of life.

19

new schools.

"F, F, W, I, C."

Sitting in the FSU Pre-Health Advising Office waiting area, I was staring at the top of my transcript printout of all my college grades thus far. These five letter grades were the first ones to appear, reflecting my first and only semester at Temple University in the Fall of 1998. It was a dismal failure. After graduating near the top of my class at BHS that previous spring, my summer break quickly transitioned to me packing my grandmother's Geo Metro with whatever items I could fit into its hatchback. Crossing over the Walt Whitman Bridge for only the second time in my life, this time felt eerily different than the first. My initial visit was with my parents: a collegiate tour of the dorms and what the school had to offer. They showed us the nicer part of Philly, and then provided us with preadmission paperwork. The application felt like an instructional how-to guide, written in a broken foreign language, to assist us with my first steps toward higher education. The year before I was offered a partial scholarship, with bolded details as to how the other part would be paid: student loans. I couldn't afford the living option advertised to us during the tour, so I opted for the Plan B package that was about twenty blocks from the school, right off Dauphin Street: my cousin Debbie's house.

Debbie was a relative on my mother's late father's side. She was a separated, middle-aged woman with two kids still living at home: Nicki, who was a fellow

1998 high school grad like myself, and Leroy, who was still in middle school, but hung out with all the other high school dropouts that failed to graduate with Nicki. She was a master seamstress, who mostly worked from home and was deeply loved in her neighborhood. Her house was a typical Philly townhome, attached to several other row houses along a narrow one-way street. The first-floor walls were all mirrored with black-and-gold trim. Stepping into her living room felt like an event, a runway show stage for both clients and visitors alike. She kindly offered me shelter in her residence; Leroy had a bottom bunk bed that I was welcome to, and her house was near the bus station that took me directly to school. The first few months were cool; however, I was starting to feel the tensions rise as the semester went on. Nicki and Leroy were very kind to me and showed me nothing but love, but I could sense Nicki tiring of Debbie's constant reminders of "See, Jimmy is going to college and doing something with his life" and how badly Leroy missed his private space. To make matters worse, three months in, with a few weeks left into the semester, Debbie pulled me to the side.

"Cousin, you know I love you and I proud of you," she said. "But I'ma keep it real... your mom hasn't paid me yet."

"Oh, I am sorry," I said nervously. "I didn't know she owed you money. I can ca—"

"Yes, she does. For you being here. Now, I know you are trying to focus on school, and I get all of that. But I got my own problems, Baby. And your mom said she was going to send some money every month and it wasn't much, but she hasn't sent any. It ain't the money, it's the principle. So, if she doesn't start sending it, I'm sorry but you will have to find some other place to stay."

"Oh... okay. I understand. I'm sorry... I... I will call her." I went up to Leroy's room, hoping he wasn't there to see me attempt to hide my tears.

Shocked, I sat on the bottom bunk bed, in the dark, and cried to myself. She was right. It was the principle. I mean, it was definitely not the money because firstly, my family didn't have any, and secondly, Joyce never told me of this financial arrangement. I was informed that Cousin Debbie was letting me stay with her out of the kindness of her heart. I later learned that Joyce promised to send Debbie $150/month for my small portion of room rent, and that Poochie told her she gave the money to me every month—so I must have kept it for myself. Embarrassed that someone gracious enough to let me stay in their home now thought I was thief, I figured it was best to just leave at the end of the month. Besides, I wasn't passing my classes anyway.

School always came easy to me. My internal motto to myself, regardless of the degree of difficulty with any subject, is that if there is a question, then there must be an answer. I could always find the answer because in the past I was always provided the tools for free. College wasn't free, though. The price tag Temple presented to me for the cost of their tools came to an impressive $3,000/month. That number was stifling; especially considering my family was living off the equivalent of approximately $12,000 for the year. I didn't have the money, but I didn't know what else to do—so I just went to school. Every day, I caught the SEPTA bus to campus, went to classes and tried to absorb lectures without books. I obviously missed homework assignments and couldn't participate in group projects. Tests days were a joke. I would stare blankly at testing sheets, nearly in tears, frozen by the dizzying reality that my idea of trying to acquire a better life for myself was spinning out of control. Unaware of how to possibly turn my situation into something meaningful, on December 4, a week before final exams, I packed up the few items I could, purchased a one-way bus ticket, and ashamedly went back to NJ. A new reality, but with similar results. I dropped out of college, one semester in, not because I couldn't handle the pressure, but simply because I couldn't afford to be in school, nor could I afford a place to stay when I wasn't.

I never showed anyone my first college report card. I felt like it wasn't fair, like it reflected more of my situation than my efforts. However, it does tell my story. It captures a moment where I was faced with the harsh reality of how success and failure both shared hard and isolated paths. You take all the credit when you're winning and carry all the blame when you lose. I buried the experience deep inside of my pride, only to be reminded of my initial collegiate failure every time someone would see me working at local jobs or ask me how school was going. Tired of making excuses for myself, and afraid of becoming the common denominator in a series of black male statistics, I eventually matriculated into a local state college, Rowan University. I was provided tuition assistance, on-campus housing allowances, and a chance to prove that my mettle wasn't broken. I fell in love (with a childhood friend from Florida), made new friends, tried to patch things up at home, and felt assured that I was finally on a path of betterment for once in my life. Eighteen months in, more confident after a few semesters of success, I again packed my bags, hugged and kissed my family on the cheeks, left school, and bought a one-way ticket out of town. This time, though, I wasn't leaving because I failed; I was leaving for a better opportunity, I believed, to win.

Leaving NJ was difficult, but I knew that staying there any longer would have made it nearly impossible to ever leave. It's not that moving to a new place would absolve me of having problems, but it would ensure any problems I encountered were specifically my own. For the all the positives I could name for my altruistic dealings back home, there were an equally exponential number of factors that were robbing me of the chance to reach my full potential. Jerald was learning that fast money was better than slow money. Jessica was pregnant and on the verge of dropping out of high school. Poochie finally started to receive her long-awaited disability funds, but the years of suffering into poorer states of health left her so debilitated that she was unable to enjoy the sporadic fruits of her perceived financial rewards. My family wasn't living month to month, we were surviving week to week. So instead of using my weekends to study and further my education, I found myself coming home to make sure "everything was okay." But they weren't. I soon realized that if I kept coming home, kept putting me second, kept losing sleep over a nightmare that seemed to be never-ending, then my dream of betterment would continue to be deferred until it eventually festered into a sore. So, I left—for myself and for love.

Yet, we were just kids, childhood figments trying to escape the riddle of the inner isolation we always felt regarding our families and upbringing. Getting married made sense, so we found a Justice of the Peace, signed a few documents and, as husband and wife, we moved into a small apartment together that she shared with her sister in Tallahassee, Florida. The challenge of trying to figure out how to be someone's husband—while starting a new life in a new place—was a whirlwind. Young and naïve, all the good things about being in love at nineteen and twenty years old made all the bad things, at first, not seem so bad. However, since this book is not about my intimate life, and to avoid misinterpreting her side of the story, I will simply say: The best part of my being married to Natalie was that, in her own way, she indirectly introduced me to "hope."

Tallahassee was a big adjustment for me. While she had her sister, all her old high school friends, and now fellow HBCU classmates who shared in her collegiate experience and could offer emotional/social support that (at that point in life) was fully difficult to appreciate, I only had her. Thus, although we lived together, our lived experiences were very much different. I rushed to Florida with the hope that it would be she and I against the world, but it quickly became she and I, in her world, against a world that could care less if I even existed. Transferring schools from state to state was not as easy as I anticipated. The core educational curricula between each school were varied. Had I tried to go directly into a four-year school, I would have had to forfeit a year and a half of the positive scholastic achievements/credits I acquired at Rowan over the last eighteen months. Tack on the wasted semester at Temple University, which was still hovering above my college transcript, I would be losing not only two years of post-high-school education, but also two years of my life. Thankfully, Florida had an archaic rule that allowed you to immediately enroll into any of its four-year state collegiate institutions if you received an associate's degree from one of its many community colleges. My second Plan B, thus, was to enroll at Tallahassee Community College, quickly obtain my AA/AS, then transition smoothly into Florida State University as a junior and complete my bachelor's degree, in a yet to be determined field of study. Easy.

Writing this all down on a scrap sheet of paper and presenting it to Natalie and her sister (my new roommate) made sense (to me at least), but that's not how life works. The apartment we stayed in was their apartment. The car that we shared, which would be necessary for me to implement this master plan, was their car. It quickly became evident that although the energy about me being there was positive, it also required a different (residential and transportation) platform, as well as additional financial backing for it all to work. Thus, I went to work. At first, I thought my job at First Union National Bank was going to be a brief aside, a quick way to make a few dollars so that I could start going to school full time. Within a few months, the reverse happened, though: School became a part-time gig and work became a full-time investment.

Wanting to prove my worth to this new family equation I was now a part of, I slaved all day at work and then took classes whenever time allowed. I was a full-time bank teller and part-time student, but at no time did I feel like myself. Night classes. TV (i.e., VHS tapes rented from the school's library) and online classes. Late nights and long mornings. I buried myself so deeply into my game plan to somehow make my "new life" work, that I failed to see how it was slowly starting to break into little pieces. When I eventually came up for air, my marriage was failing, my credit score was in the basement (this was around the time when I learned of Poochie's ill-adventurous endeavors), my social life was growing but it, too, was just a collection of a few coworkers and people I superficially met in some of my classes. I couldn't afford to go back home, but all the bad news back home (Jessica was struggling with another pregnancy; Jerald was imprisoned for illegal activities; Joyce's failing health was steadily worsening) was finding its way back to me. I don't remember if I was depressed or if I was just numb to the feeling of always being a few steps behind. It felt like fate was prompting me to not forget that my idea of "making it to the top" was still not very far from the bottom. And right before everything came crashing down, with my reflection in the mirror sadly staring back at a man who was broken but still pieced together enough to hide it from the world, I noticed that Pam McCully was wearing a new, brighter shade of lipstick.

"Oooou, what's the special occasion?" I asked as I emptied the mail from my courier bag on her desk.

"We..." finishing her makeup application in a small desk mirror, "just got accredited!!" Pam said with a large smile.

She worked in the Accounts Receivable department for FSU PIMS program. This program was designed to provide the first year of medical training for nontraditional medical students, who then transferred to University of Florida's formal School of Medicine for the remainder of their course work and graduate education. The focus was to increase the number of practitioners who had a passion to serve in primary care fields in underserved areas. Its decades-long track record was a testament to its success; however, as Pam described, new legislation was being put forth to transition FSU PIMS program to a formal College of Medicine. This next step in accreditation was the final step in going from a feeder program of medical professionals to the first medical school to be established in the country in over twenty years. My only affiliation with it all was Pam. I had a second, government funded work-study job, as a campus mail courier, and Pam's office was on my daily route.

Our conversation that day sparked my curiosity about this "medical school" thing. Always gifted in science and math, I gravitated to the field of Biology because it both challenged and fascinated me, but I wasn't quite sure what I would "be when I grew up." The irony, though, was that I was already grown. My marriage was broken but I was still married, still had bills and daily life responsibilities. I never fully committed to a "career" path, which was becoming a daily argument between Natalie and me. She was well established with her plans in the world of business and finance, having completed multiple externships and having been awarded numerous scholarships for her scholastic achievements. Although I fully encouraged her and felt like her biggest cheerleader at times, her support of my efforts felt mundane and limited by both her disbelief in my ability to establish a path and my fear of never being able to create one.

My lack of "having a solid plan" was more out of uncertainty and limited clarity about what it meant to be successful (in any fashion), as opposed to a dearth of drive or initiative. I wanted to be *somebody*, but was so used to being a *nobody*, taking care of *everybody*, and not being encouraged by *anybody*, that I was merely excited about the fact that I was moving forward in my life. I, however, was naïve to how important it was to also have some sense of direction. I thought about becoming a teacher, a chemist, a researcher, or even a pharmacist. Physical trainer or physical therapist were terms I heard classmates toss around, but I was too ashamed to ask more questions about it all, afraid that my limited knowledge would be exposed. Equally, I was embarrassed that my "taking classes" without a formal plan would be ridiculed outside of my home life as well. One day, after a heated discussion, I remember Natalie mentioning I should go to "this guy's wife" who she did some volunteer work with, Mrs. Thelsa Anderson, an academic advisor for pre-health students. I eventually looked her up online, called her office, and made an advising appointment. Writing down the time and contact information, I noticed that her location was not too far from Pam McCully's—at the new College of Medicine.

Her office was small, and cluttered. The PIMs program was housed in an old high school that was on the FSU campus, so many of the administration offices were just restructured classrooms. Her desk was filled with tons of medical school brochures and MCAT preparatory test booklets. A large computer screen that she stared at as she asked me questions partially obscured my view of her facial expressions. There were a lot of fliers about MAPS (a pre-health organization I heard friends in classes speak about) and SSTRIDE (a program I heard she was spearheading that was a pipeline for high school students to become medical professionals) piled on her desk and on the seat next to me. A thick Caribbean accent lingered on her words when she spoke. There was a motherly pace to her tone, as if she was busy (multitasking and such) but didn't make me feel as if she was in a rush. I carried on about my academic path; I was careful not to sound like I was making excuses. Embarrassed that my transcript had so many credits without any form of direction, I started to conceal my lack of confidence by blurting out various career fields I had been considering.

"So... ummm... I was thinking about maybe becoming some type of therapists, like physical or occupational. I'm not sure." The latter field was one I quickly looked up before coming to the appointment.

"Hmmm.... I see," she said while slowing down her finger clicking on the mouse she was holding the entire time.

There was an awkward moment of silence, a pause I was used to. A part of me was waiting for that feeling to arrive: the one where all the good things that can possibly happen to me suddenly disappear and make room for all the bad things. My entire life was a series of disappointments. Here I was again, I thought, with my grip on this newest attempt to avoid the inevitability of failure, slowly slipping away with only a conversational pause to disrupt the impact of the fall. However, something else happened when she spoke again; something magical. All my negative intuitions, thoughts, and feelings about what I could be, and what I was destined to become, instantly came to a halt. For the first time, in my adult life, and in a long, long time, I felt like someone genuinely believed in me. Someone looked at my collection of small victories and not only saw the battle within my choices, but also the reason I was at war. Someone saw the passionate efforts in my chaos and the coming of a rainbow in my perpetual storm.

The question she asked wasn't laced with the undertones of doubt, nor with an aim to dispel the dream I held onto of becoming something more than a collection of decent grades under the first five letters (F, F, W, I, C) of my academic transcripts. I could sense, immediately, that she knew I wasn't in her office to prove myself to her, or anyone else, but rather to tap into this insatiable drive I had to make sure my life made a difference. That moment, in her office, didn't merely change my life, it made everything I felt about my life suddenly change. In that moment, it all instantly made sense, when she turned from her computer screen, clasped her hands together on her desk and asked me:

"Have you ever thought about becoming a doctor?"

20

doctored life.

B efore my mother passed away in 2013, she and I made peace. All the invisible scars from my childhood and residual stains of our broken bond, each echoed in the emotions of unhealed traumas, were buried along with the hatchet that cut into the creases of our love. The year before her death, I was able to send Ella on a trip for her to finally "getaway." She was my mother's primary caretaker at this point, as she was now an amputee and dialysis patient from all the years of unchecked diabetes, reduced to a fraction of the large and physically imposing woman she was in my youth. I flew to NJ for the week (ironically, around Mother's Day weekend) and relieved Ella of her healthcare and provider duties. Each day, I assisted in transporting my mother to and from various stores. We went to her dialysis sessions and doctors' appointments as well, where she proudly showed off her "own doctor (son)" to all the local medical staff, who at this point considered her family.

Most of our car rides were silent, but I could feel the radiance of pride emanating from her in the passenger seat. There wasn't much to say, but the calm between us said a lot. There was no anger anymore, no teenage resentment twisted into a tightened thread of pain, needling its way into our bond. Over the last few years of her life, she would sporadically call me, apologizing for things in the past, rambling and confusing her words and stories. I would acknowledge her in those moments, reminding her that the past is the past, but I understood why she called. As we get older and consider our mortality, we tend to extend the grace we never afforded ourselves to those who we may have robbed of it as well. Joyce's apologies were as much about her making peace with her past, as they were about she and I making peace with our own. I never really felt like her son in my youth, but during those last few car rides with her, she felt very much like my mom. One time, after I finished bathing and clothing her, and emptying her bedside commode, she started to cry.

"Mom, what's wrong?"

"I just feel bad, Jimmy. I feel really bad. I wasn't the best mom, but I promise I tried; I tried really hard. And I feel bad that you have to come here and clean me up and bathe me. It's embarrassing because... I wasn't the best mom, but I tried," she proclaimed, as more and more tears ran down her face.

Hugging her, I reassured her that I loved her deeply and that I truly believed I was where I existed in life because she did exactly that: she tried. My statements weren't falsely noted; I fervently meant every word. For all my successes at that point, I never labeled them as some grand extension from a previous point of failure. As much as she was present and partially to blame for some of the lowest times in my life, I still credit her for not bailing ship or giving up altogether. The biggest lesson in life that she taught me is that, most of the time, people aren't failing to live up to our expectations, but rather they are simply doing the best that they can. That best may fall short of what we deem to be necessary to our vision of betterment; however, the onus is ours to make sense of it all. Joyce gave me the best she could possibly give me—a chance at more life—and I am glad that I had to chance to reflect that with her before she ultimately lost hers.

Before my grandmother suffered a similar fate in 2015, her cancer abruptly exploded to an aggressive form and metastasized throughout her body. I remember receiving the phone call while on my pediatric anesthesia rotation. She noted that her oncologist stated she could continue chemo and possibly live another six months, or she could go home with hospice.

"What do you think I should do, Moss?" she asked, her voice weakened from weight loss and the ill effects of her body waging war against the assertiveness of a highly malignant cancer.

"I don't know, Grandma.... I know you don't like hospitals and the chemo will assuredly keep you in and out of the hospitals over those last six months." I tried to hide my fear of losing her with a strength I borrowed from the hospital wall I was leaning against. She saw through it all, though.

"Boy don't be getting all worked up for nothing. All that sadness won't do me no good. You stop that. But you right. I'ont wanna be stuck up here for nothing. So, I'll tell the hospice people I want to go home."

And that's what she did. She went back to her apartment, with hospice, and five days later, with me and her entire family at her side, she went home. Her skin was still smooth and only wrinkled from years of victorious laughter in the face of pain. Her joy was radiant. It was rich and pushed away the stain of poverty whenever it tried to steal away our inner promise. For so long, I leaned on her calm demeanor and wise, analogous views on life, love, and so many other things. Yet, in the moment where I wanted her to lean on me, for healing and for possibly more time on Earth, she was still "Grandma Ella". She was still somehow remaining a pillar of comfort for me, letting me drink from her endless pool of perseverance. She was passing the torch to me, as well, making me promise to be the lifeline she was for our family whenever life tried to drown us with waves of fear. Kneeling on the floor next to her bed, I kissed her and held her hand as she took her last breath, peaceful and no longer tired. I could sense that she understood what her life's purpose was and that she felt her task was completed.

My grandmother once told me, "Jimmy, you are my gift to the world. A lotta people can say they made a lotta things, but they can never say they made a 'Jimmy Moss'... but I can."

She followed that comment with a deep, heartfelt laughter, one that I hear etched in the vibrant amusement of my two little daughters, Jayla and Amaya, who never formally met her but definitely carry the joy of her life in their mannerisms. Before she passed away, I sent Ella on trips she dreamed of taking, bought her cars she spoke of driving, and was even able to cover most of her bills so that she could finally enjoy the fruits of all the seeds she sowed into the many fields of my life. A part of me wishes I had more time with her on Earth, but another part of me fully understands that the time I did have with her was more than enough to convey the message she wanted to deliver: I am a truly gift, not merely to this world but also to my own.

Before we lost our parents, my relationship with Jerald and Jessica was still fractured. We share a similar past, but our life choices pointed us in different directions. It would be easy for someone on the outside to quickly glance at the three of us and make assumptions about who was, or who is, more successful. However, they would be mistaken by a blinded idea of success. We each survived a childhood that was riddled with disruption and ran rampant without a developed measure of balance. How we individually manage stress, cope with loss, and deal with outpourings of love is varied, but it would be an egregious error to not assess our future selves without considering our previous lived experiences. As adults, we must face the blame of any actions we allow to reflect our character; thus, it is paramount that each of us make peace with all the wrongs we feel were unfairly assigned to us in our youth. I offer them a portion of my grace. Moreover, I also hold them to a higher standard because the same valor they used to survive the hell they endured in our childhood is more than enough to assist them in their efforts to create a better heaven for their futures. This book is my way of making sense of it all for myself, and if it offers them a sampling of examples of how to continue doing the same for themselves, then I will consider these pages a success.

Before I applied for my fellowship at Mass General Hospital, I noticed the insignia accompanying the program's application: Harvard Medical School. The program was included on the list of potential ones I was considering, but seeing the word "Harvard" bolded in its trademark crimson resulted in my crossing it off the list. Because, I mean, it's Harvard, the gold standard of academic excellence. Up to that point, I completed many professional milestones, and my curriculum vitae (resume) was becoming respectfully extended, but there was something inside of me that still felt like it was all a fluke. My board certification in internal medicine and being on the brink of becoming board certified in anesthesiology was a feat that most physicians could never declare. However, even at my highest point of professional attainment, having reached for stars that would have escaped the imagination of a much younger version of myself, the possibility of falling from my heights was an immediate fear. Even with all my accumulating degrees on the wall, there remained a degree of doubt in whether I was actually anything more than just a poor kid from the hood. But I still applied.

Surprisingly, I received an email, which I initially thought was a kindhearted rejection letter, inviting me to interview for a candidacy seat for MGH's 2016 incoming class for their Anesthesiology Critical Care Fellowship. My initial excitement was quickly calmed by the fact that this was merely an interview; yet, in my mind, receiving the invite was proof that I had already won. In fact, during my interview on their campus with Dr. Sheri Berg, I expressed the same sentiments when she asked me, "Why should we accept you into our program?"

"With all due respect, Dr, Berg. I have already won. I never would have imagined in my wildest dreams of being here... in this seat... sitting across from a Harvard Medical School associate professor, talking with her about her love for bulldogs and my possibly becoming a future fellow in their program. People like me, from where I am from, don't make it this far. This feels like a dream, a story ending chapter for a book that maybe I should write one day. I mean, I went from being homeless to graduating college to going to medical school to being on the verge of completing my second residency program... and now I have a chance, which is all we can ask for in life... a chance, of finishing the end of this chapter in my life... with you asking me why you should accept me in a Harvard Medical school training program. I would love to come here. It would be a dream come true for a dream I never actually had. I actually was never going to apply, but I did. I didn't allow fear and self-doubt to prevent me from applying and that makes me a winner. And if your program would like to have another winner in your long (storied) lists of winning candidates, then I feel I would be a perfect fit. But regardless if you accept me or not, with all due respect, I already won."

Before I became a biological father of my own, I was blessed with the chance to become a father through love. The family that Amy extended to me, included two additions to my life, Tamara and Sierra, that have widened my lens of what fatherhood truly means. My struggles with parenting have been marred by not having a father of my own. Initially, I spent more time trying to not be like the men I vowed to never become, than I did simply being the man I was already becoming. Accepting that I was not merely unlike them, but completely my own collection of lived choices (and consequences), allowed me to flourish at showing my girls love as I knew it. I have learned to be openly joyful, expressively concerning, painstakingly human, and, more importantly, very much myself. What my girls see is a flawed man, but one who isn't afraid of trying. They are witnesses to my successes, and now are privy to the primal core—and most of the beginnings—of my many failures. I am not ashamed to hug them in public, love them in a fashion that may cause them embarrassing moments, or even show them my tears when life has burdened me beyond my strength. What I offer them, with this book, is hopefully a larger and clearer vision of their dad, a better understanding of my passions, and another chance to personally observe how to (somehow) take a broken life and compile it into something worthy of calling healed.

We all have a few stories to tell, and this book is a small collection of some of mine. It's not perfect, but neither am I. When Mrs. Anderson asked me if I ever considered becoming a physician almost two decades ago, I never imagined that my not having an answer in that moment was truly the dividing line between the person I was and the man I am still becoming. If there's anything I have gained from my experiences it is that life isn't about the decisions you make, but more so about how you respond to those decisions. Nothing makes absolute sense when we first venture into it; our purpose is usually driven by hindsight and reflection. Before we take steps toward our future, we lean on steps we have taken before. Sometimes we leap, but even leaping only occurs when you have learned how to jump. The landing isn't always perfect, but sometimes—if you happen to fall—you are able to get up, look around, dust yourself off, and gain more insight about who you are, what motivates you, and if that last step (or leap) was worth trying it all again.

This is my leap. It is my hope that when this effort lands in my daughters' hands one day, they will have a clearer picture of one outlook about life. I have more stories to tell them, and, hopefully, more stories to make. If this story offers them a better appreciation of the man who loves them and how his approach to life's challenges was managed with both fear and curiosity, as well as with courage and doubt, then maybe they will take the pieces they deem suitable for their lives and be able to doctor together a better life for themselves.

The End.

afterword:

So yes, I wrote a book. It took me a while for obvious reasons, but the primary reason was I never wrote a book before. I always hear about people venturing into the literary world, posting online via social media that they wrote a book, or will write one. My immediate thought is, *"Wow, that's awesome!"* and *"Congratulations"*. However, after the hoopla fades and I have their book in hand, I realize that most people didn't actually write a book, but rather jotted their thoughts down on paper, printed it out with a few illustrative components, and sold me said book for a nominal (profitable) fee. It always makes me wonder how "true authors" feel about this process; laypeople jumping into their field, headfirst, with the notion that compiling a novel is a simple task. Just open a Word document, start typing, add some page numbers, use thesarus.com to expand their lexicon, and then google how to get a book published. Done.

I feel such an approach devalues the actual process of creating a literary work. There are a lot of amazing writers; individuals who have spent decades, and hundreds of thousands of hours, of their waking (and sleeping) lives crafting new worlds, and even languages, within the framework of pages. Their minds are epicenters of vocabulary greatness; context masterminds, whose thoughts are scripted into movies and theatrical events that utterly change how we view the world around us. For some, they have also aided in evolving these worlds, constructing imaginary dimensions out of a tangible collection of words. It makes me wonder how they (probably) feel when someone mentions "I'm writing book". Is there a hint of encouraged excitement in their tone, understanding that they too were in a place where they were non-famous first-time authors? Or do they cloak their cynicism with cautious smiles and tilted heads, as if to say, "Oh really? Ha! Good luck with that" (*and don't send me a copy*)?

Writing is both an escape and an adventure. Although we often find ourselves connecting to groups of people who share similar fictional affinities, the quest is more individual than it is collective. However, outlining these audacious movements and novelistic journeys for people to follow requires a lot of effort and sacrifice. It's a task I would like to assume that most successful writers take quite seriously, and I liken it to my primary profession. As a physician, I am often bombarded, and bumrushed, at hospital doors by well-read WebMD clinicians who swear their blog research trumps my six diplomas and nearly twenty years of medical training. I hear them, but find myself not listening to a word they're saying. I smile, and, for good measure, I also tilt my head.

You can't google "how to be a doctor" and then actually become one. You can't find intricate details of what I do on any website, not even the scholarly ones. Medicine isn't a collection of math formulas, red or blue pill decisions, and matrix algorithms that are easily sorted out. Nothing ever matches, and rarely is anything about disease, death and dying easily explainable. A patient, as noted by Dr. John Barber Hickam, has the right to have "as many diseases as he damn well pleases". My tasks only start with identifying these problems (diseases and syndromes), and truly never ends with me writing a prescription, or performing a procedure, to treat them. The element of humanism that is stitched into every fabric of my patient encounters is hidden beneath the creases of held hands and outlining realistic expectations in the face of a fading hope. The art of medicine is not a literary one, but one that requires time, energy, and patience. It requires not merely knowing that the tears streaming down my neck, from a dying patient's wife, as I hug her after losing him during a prolonged cardiac resuscitation attempt, may come from the distant interlobular ducts of the lacrimal gland, but also from someplace else. It requires a steady voice, a calming hand, and a soothing demeanor. It also requires a rich understanding that simply being knowledgeable, or searching google, will never replace the true compassion of another human trying (their best) to avoid the sting that death is attempting to inflict onto another.

Writing is easy, but writing a book requires a deeply committed effort. It's an art. When I decided to sit down and write this book, the challenges were far greater than my desire to write it. I wanted to tell my story and not perform a disservice to true authors—so I did some work. I read other great pieces. I listened to dozens of books on Audible. I read short stories and poems; I even tried to learn new words and better analogies. I ingratiated myself to the process of creating *art*. My aim was to ensure that if this book ever landed in the hands of a great writer, their smiles would not be laced with cynicism, and their head tilts will be positioned in a manner of curiosity for more—and not less. I approached it like I approach medicine, with discipline, thoroughness, open-mindedness, and honesty. I wanted this book to capture my human experience. It was constructed, thus, in a fashion that would convey how I feel when I am holding a sick patient's hand, when the only things standing between them and myself is not only the unpredictability of death, but also the hope (and curiosity) of more life.

I hope you enjoyed this first attempt. I have more stories and more moments that I hold within my imagination, too many to fit into the fingertips of these pages. I struggle with how to share them, or even if I should. However, I promise that if I ever make an effort to formulate them into a second book, I won't type into my Google search: *how to write a sequel*.